I0067453

Your Recipe for Financial Success

Cookbook Investing

A great investment strategy is like a great recipe. It should be simple, easy to follow, and produce consistent results.

Guy Terrell
Jack Trammell

High Tide
Publications, Inc.
It's never too late to write

Copyright © Guy Terrell and Jack Trammell
May 2025.
All rights reserved.
ISBN: 978-1-962935-11-1

Published by High Tide Publications, Inc.
www.Hightidepublications.com
Deltaville, Virginia

Thank you for choosing this authorized edition of *Cookbook Investing*. At High Tide, our mission is to discover, promote, and publish the work of talented authors over 50. Your support by purchasing an authorized copy is crucial in helping us bring their work to you.

Respecting copyright law by refraining from reproducing or scanning any part without our permission is not just about obeying the law, but also about respecting the authors' rights and enabling us to continue supporting them. Your decision to purchase an authorized edition is not only a personal choice, but a valuable contribution to the authors and the entire publishing process. It allows us to bring their work to you and to a wider community of readers.

Your support in our mission to bring the work of our authors to a wider audience is deeply appreciated. Thank you for choosing to purchase an authorized edition.

Edited by Cindy L. Freeman (cindylfreeman.com)
Book design by Firebellied Frog Graphic Design

Visit the author's website at www.Cookbookinvesting.com.

Dedicated to

Realistic and Persistent Dreamers—Like You

Table of Contents

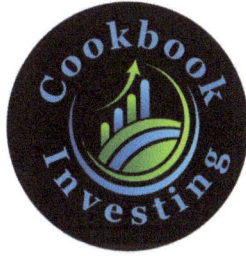

Part III - Adding Extra Courses to the Meal After Two or Three Years of Investing

Preface

Welcome! Come in and look around. We have put together a "cookbook" of our investment successes and failures to provide steps for anyone to invest in the stock market. We think investing is like cooking. In the culinary world, you will find a handful of elites—famous, sought-after chefs—but the rest of us have full-time obligations. That means we pursue our culinary skills whenever we can. The same is true in investing. The tycoons of Wall Street and the licensed experts invest as a profession, but the rest of us must pursue it whenever we can fit it into our busy lives.

The satisfaction of that first bite into something delicious you made in your kitchen is how it feels to see a stock you picked pay a dividend for the first time and show up in your account balance.

The world of personal investing is as accessible as the world of learning new recipes. Things don't always go according to plan, which is not a reason to give up or dwell on disappointment.

It takes resolve when the stocks you own decline as will happen from time to time. The reason not to panic or sell is because fluctuation creates new opportunities. Stocks often go up or down for no obvious or discernable reason. Over the years, you will want to add shares of stock you already own or pick up shares in companies that are dynamic and growing the same way you might repeat successful recipes in the kitchen while also trying something new. Many professional investors forage for stocks and then abandon them. Most of us do not have the luxury of investing that way. Instead, we have other endeavors and interests to pursue, but we still want our savings to work alongside our primary pursuits to build multiple streams of income.

Most days the stock market moves very little. So, it is important to always be invested. The market goes up big only a few times a year, but at its heart it is a natural system that moves upward over time. As companies create new products or increase sales, your stock will go up. Plus, population and demand normally increase roughly two percent each year.

Recently, Artificial Intelligence stocks have been on fire. If you do not own any of the stocks that are going up every day, you might think you must buy something, or you'll be left behind. This is known as FOMO—Fear of Missing Out. Should you rush out and buy stock in Nvidia, Microsoft, Apple, and Micron Technology or one of the other stocks closely related to the surge of interest in Artificial Intelligence? The answer is no. Wait a little while, form a plan based on research, and act with caution. Like becoming an accomplished chef, it is not luck as much as it is a process.

As we were writing this book, many popular stocks took a serious beating in a market swing. (In a later chapter you will see charts of stocks from those days as an example.) Stocks, fortunately, are on sale every business day. There will always be another buying opportunity. Good companies stay good for decades, so you must be immune to emotions that could sidetrack your plans. The noise from websites, television, financial advisers, banks, brokers, and even well-meaning friends is deafening. We will show you how to develop your own inner voice then listen to it and focus on one ingredient at a time.

If we could tell you only one thing at the outset, it is this: save modest amounts of money, research good companies, then buy stock in those companies. Do it again and again. Some of the stocks will grow spectacularly (you only need to find one or two), and some will not immediately increase in value, but continue to follow a buy-and-hold strategy over time. Stocks, like bread rising, need time to mature. Your persistence and patience will reap the benefits of stock ownership. We will show you in this book how to implement a successful overall strategy.

Whether you're just beginning to invest or already own some stocks, a basic requirement is adaptability. When the environment changes, you must adapt to the new circumstances. You don't need to change your investments or objectives every day like changing clothes. Don't sell *your* stock because an analyst or journalist casts aspersions on the stock of a company you own. Warren Buffett said to think of buying shares of stock as if you were buying the entire company. Some investments you hold through good times and uncertain times. New ideas come to you and new products are created. Your job as an investor is to consistently add money and purchase additional shares of companies you already own or stock of companies you have recently discovered.

You will have no trouble knowing when to sell these stocks. Julius Westheimer, who was a frequent guest on Louis Rukeyser's show, *Wall Street Week*, on public television many years ago, said it best, "Buy when you have money. Sell when you need money." Companies do not open, close, or abandon their operations each night or close on the weekend. Investors sometimes sell companies on the spur of the moment when fear or uncertainty reign. One day a stock might take a steep fall. In July 2024, when Novo Nordisk reported a decline in sales, not only did its stock decline but investors assumed that the same fate would befall Eli Lilly and Company whose product line is similar to Novo Nordisk's. Lilly's stock went down, but because the company reported superior earnings, its stock recovered quickly. Do not allow yourself to be whipsawed by rumors or emotions. Novo Nordisk similarly recovered after a few days. Your stocks, too, will likely recover even if they go down. When you buy a stock, you are investing your hard-earned money in your own optimism, creativity, and courage.

> *No magic takes places in our investing lives. Sometimes we get lucky and pick up a stock that goes up like a hot-air balloon. Most of the time, however, slow and steady wins the race. Investors have to have a degree of ice-water in their veins like a general who knows an enemy army is up ahead. When the stock market goes against you, and it will, dig in your heels, grasp your sword, and hold your position. No matter the condition of the stock market, you must always be adding money.*
>
> *A quote attributed to Nathan Mayer Rothchild, founder of NM Rothchild & Sons, says "buy at the sound of the cannon, sell at the sound of trumpets." It's not always that way though. Day in and day out the stock market barely moves. Just keep doing the same thing: Buy when you have money, watch for bargains, and sell when you need money. All the rest is noise.*

And when you buy stock, you are purchasing the gifts and talents of every person who works at that company. If the company did well in its on-going operations yesterday, it is likely to exceed expectations today, tomorrow, and every day after. In 1998-1999, Amazon stock sank with the rest of the internet-based companies. Some investors sold their stock at a tremendous loss. Those who didn't went on to recoup their losses and make spectacular gains. The reason the stock of Berkshire Hathaway has done so well is that the managers of Berkshire Hathaway (historically Warren Buffet and Charlie Munger) bought good companies and supported the managers of those companies.

We do not believe you can use stocks as a quick recipe for riches. But, in time, you can become an accomplished chef. It takes patience, consistency, and persistence. Generally, any modest collection of stocks will likely increase in value. Your job is to hold the stocks you pick and purchase more of them while simultaneously adding companies you discover. We will show you actual screenshots of an account belonging to a close friend. This account has risen for more than fifteen years. We will share "recipes" to help you create your own successful portfolio.

There exists a dubious parallel universe where people are trying to find ways to buy only stocks whose prices are rising. We wish them luck. We have learned through experience that the "fast money" approach is not the best approach. Peter Lynch said it best, "It takes years, not months, to produce big results."

Only in the long run will a stock show its true character. This is not to discourage you or make you afraid. Personal investing is accessible and manageable for anyone. Just realize that what you think will happen often doesn't occur in the short term; we don't include any microwave recipes. Look at a chart of the entire stock market over many decades. There are peaks and valleys, but generally the market will carry your stock and everyone else's up in value.

This book is the result of a five-year research effort. We researched companies, bought their shares, lost revenue sometimes, and gained other times during the last five years. We are excited to share the fruits from that labor and welcome you to the stock market kitchen!

Introduction

Why We Wrote this Book

It always seems impossible until it is done.

—Nelson Mandela

America is on sale today at a discount compared to what its value will be in ten or fifteen years. No one knows for certain which stocks will outperform over the next decade, but there are hints everywhere. At the roulette table you do not know which number will be the winner on the next turn, so you place bets on several numbers. This is not to say the stock market is "just another form of gambling" as we heard from our elders who lived through the Great Depression. Rather, it's to say you must do research and then buy several of your best ideas because some of them will be gigantic winners, and occasionally one will be a loser. Investing is not like the Kentucky Derby where you will see the result in a short time. This is a marathon you will run continually your whole life—what you might end up passing on to your heirs.

Think of this book as the door to a more secure life for you and your family that only you can manage. It fills a long-vacant niche in the world of financial advice that mainly targets and markets to those who already have wealth. You can use this book as a step-by-step cookbook with ideas and strategies that will enable you to manage your own money as your own financial adviser or Master Chef. Wealth management companies can't make money from people without substantial assets already. Millions of ordinary Americans should have access to similar resources in the world of personal investing even if they're not rich. Here is your own "cookbook" with "recipes" that will guide you to accomplish your goals. You will learn everything from specific terminology and techniques to psychology and mindset training. It will help to demystify many processes that have been inaccessible to millions of Americans: college-age investors; elderly citizens with some money to diversify; young parents; and perhaps most importantly, people who for various cultural and economic reasons have not felt the market was accessible to them. We want to show you how to become your own "chef" and investment adviser. We hope this book can make a difference in long-term economic success for you and your family.

You Can Start Small

We created a new account with $100 last year (2024) to show you how it can be done. Near the end of the year, it looked like this:

Symbol	Description ▲	Quantity	Price	$ Chg	Day's Price % Chg	Value	Day's Value Change $	Unrealized Gain/Loss $ Chg	% Chg
HEES	H AND E EQUIP SVCS INC	7	$51.86	+$0.34	+0.66%	$361.62	+$2.38	+$21.31	+6.26%
MU	MICRON TECHNOLOGY INC	5	$101.28	-$1.26	-1.23%	$506.40	-$6.30	+$66.39	+15.09%
SRPT	SAREPTA THERAPEUTICS I	2	$117.00	-$2.72	-2.27%	$234.00	-$5.44	-$5.22	-2.18%
STLA	STELLANTIS NV	5	$13.3850	+$0.2250	+1.71%	$66.93	+$1.13	-$2.72	-3.91%
SMCI	SUPER MICRO COMPUTER	2	$47.58	+$2.23	+4.92%	$95.16	+$4.46	+$3.11	+3.38%
Balances									
Money accounts	ML DIRECT DEPOSIT PROG	228	$1.00	$0.00	0.00%	$228.00	$0.00	--	--
Cash balance						-$209.24			
Pending activity						$0.00			
Total						$1,282.87	-$3.77	+$82.87	+7.02%

CMA-Edge 57X-13R38 — Value $1,282.87 — Day's Value Change -$3.77 ▼ -0.25% — Unrealized Gain/Loss +$82.87 ▲ +7.02%

Read your portfolio story

Select view Standard ▼ Customize view — View Tax Lot Details

Warren Buffett said in a YouTube video:

Big opportunities in life must be seized. We don't do many things. [We don't act as often as we should when opportunity is right in front of us.] *When we get an opportunity to do something that's right and big we've got to do it.*

We added $100 a month on average. We will explain how to select stocks. The key is to deliberately decide to hold them for a longer period than we have been told to keep a stock. We are not traders and don't blindly follow the crowd.

Another Portfolio Of Ours That Is Older

Individual Brokerage -6133 Show number			Net Account Value		$9,842.93
			Day's Gain		$63.61 (0.65%)

You don't have a beneficiary for your account.   Show more
Add beneficiary | Set reminder ⌄

⌄ Portfolio snapshot | Open orders ( ) | Quick links ⤵

Top Movers (6)   Portfolio News

Symbol		Change %	Last Price $	Change $	Day's Gain $
PWP ⓘ	Trade	4.22%	$20.77	$0.84	$21.01
MOD ⓘ	Trade	1.82%	$134.92	$2.15	$86.00
OWL ⓘ	Trade	1.20%	$20.80	$0.25	$7.35
D ⓘ	Trade	-0.74%	$56.39	-$0.42	-$33.60
NVDA ⓘ	Trade	-0.72%	$131.83	-$0.96	-$19.20
APA ⓘ	Trade	0.17%	$26.31	$0.05	$2.25

6 Total | View full portfolio   Partially Delayed quotes as of Oct 09, 2024, 1:30 PM ET ⓘ

What We Are Not

Investorpedia.com states on their site the following:

> *It's imperative for young adults and professionals to start investing early. One of the main reasons for doing so is to obtain the power of compound interest. By holding long-term investments, one can allow his or her assets to generate more returns. Investing just a few years earlier could translate into tens of thousands, if not hundreds of thousands of additional funds [dollars] for your retirement nest egg.*

We whole-heartedly agree with this statement.

They then list several books every young investor should read. They wrap up the article with the admonition to find a suitable financial adviser. We disagree and want to promote the idea that anyone who has worked and built up even modest savings can become their own financial adviser. For a small portfolio, hiring a financial adviser creates unnecessary overhead. Most financial websites provide information that, while supportive of your objectives, suggests you turn your money over to them to manage for a fee. It may be a viable strategy for some, but even small fees on a large amount of Assets Under Management [AUM is the term you will see on many websites] produce a sizable income for financial advisers. This is not the only pathway available to you. Instead, you can succeed on your own.

If you are rich, you have several sets of assets you can select from—real estate, bonds, savings, stocks, and even art. We are only going to focus on selecting stocks. With stocks you can find abundant information that enables you to spread your available money among several equities. If your portfolio grows to $100,000 or more by following your investment ideas, then indeed you may have to seek professional advice. We met a man who built a $4,000,000 portfolio of stocks and bonds on his own. He was careful, thoughtful, and methodical, buying only stocks that he understood. It was based on his core belief that a portfolio must generate income as well as growth. After his death, his family sought professional management to preserve what he had built since none of them desired to study and maintain a portfolio of individual stocks. Building your own portfolio requires serious scrutiny.

We do not propose following the advertised strategies that are rampant across the internet espousing proprietary models that will soon make you a millionaire. Flashy ads may say they can identify stocks that will go up 1,000 percent. Or they have a daily email that provides a strategy that will make you thousands each day. Maybe some of these methods work but beware that they charge substantial initial amounts. We think you'd be better off investing what you might pay them into two or three stocks with reasonable upside potential. The stock market itself is a man-made system that has evolved into a magnificent and powerful force. Thousands of people comment, write, and earn their living from commentary and advice on the stock market every day. They are trying to find new ways—or at least define the current ways—that the market operates. You and I cannot hope to understand all the gyrations of the stock market. Just know they exist. The market has been deeply studied and dissected. Learn from what others know, but don't let it put you off since you can't know as much as all the "professionals" know. You can make money on your own or by using what you learn from those same professionals.

What We Are

Our approach is different. *You* have *your* best interests at heart better than anyone else. You don't need to interview yourself to discover if your approach matches your goals. We will provide tools and examples to use to become your own financial adviser. We have examined our own mistakes and successes and will share them with you. Consider this a cookbook, with recipes (stock selections) for investors like you at your current level, especially if you fall into demographics that traditionally have been left out of American economic success.

This book is intended to reach those who are willing to develop an active interest in managing some portion of their own finances. We suggest leaving alone the 401k associated with your work, letting financial establishments already set up with your employer handle it. At the same time, we encourage you to set aside additional funds to invest parallel to your 401k investments.

Other books and websites say, "Subscribe to our service and we'll tell you what to buy so you can become rich like we are." If you see those types of advertisements don't walk but run away from their enticements. There may be some good ones, but they still require significant fees.

We wrote this book for ourselves and for you. Our portfolios are not as large as we had hoped at our ages. Often when needs arose, we dipped into our portfolios to cover unexpected demands such as a new heat pump, a new roof, or to help a relative. Still, we have experienced success, and we will share both our successes and our failures with you. What we discovered is that success occurs over time and begins in the mind. You must apply discipline to each area, your finances, and your mind. If you don't know who you are, Wall Street is a terrible place to find out. If you tend to beat yourself up over past mistakes, investing on your own may not be the place for you. Peter Lynch in his book *One Up on Wall Street* describes the temperament required for investing:

> *Before you think about buying stocks, you ought to have made some basic decisions about the market, about how much you trust corporate America, ... and about how you will react to sudden, unexpected, and severe drops in price. ... if you are undecided and lack conviction, then you are a potential market victim, who abandons all hope and reason at the worst moment and sells out at a loss. ... Ultimately it is not the stock market nor even the companies themselves that determine an investor's fate. It is the investor.*

Going forward, we urge you to stop reviewing the financial decisions that haven't worked. Use rearview mirrors only when you drive. Toss out any mistakes like an old rug. We want to encourage you to invest. We want to stand by your side. Additionally, don't compare your stock selections or asset accumulations to others. There will always be someone else who bought Nvidia or Apple or Microsoft long before you even thought about owning them. Others will have more to invest or even get a cheaper price when they purchase stock. Managing your money and investing in the long run is not a competition.

This is our fourth book together. In the process of working on those other projects we began to talk about things that matter to us. We found we both owned individual stocks, not just mutual funds. We had been investing for many years and wanted to share what we learned. We both had times in the past when for various reasons we had to sell a portion of our portfolios to send children to school, purchase or repair homes, and for unexpected living expenses. Those were good reasons to have our own money set aside outside of our retirement funds. As we wrote this book, we laid out our ideas presenting various real and hypothetical situations and asked ourselves what we should be doing.

The Single Most Important Stock Marker

The one thing we wish we had known many years ago is what is the best indicator for a stock? The answer is a consistent (not dramatic) rise in its price indicated by a rising chart. There are many well-known examples such as Apple and Microsoft. But there are other excellent examples such as Welltower and Owens-Corning.

In a report by Merrill Lynch on Well Tower, they mention that one of the oft-overlooked aspects of a company's financial performance is their culture. The first step is to look for charts of companies that resemble these.

We reproduce the charts taken from *NASDAQ.com* of Welltower, Costco, and Owens-Corning on the following page.

> While some of these charts will have a sawtooth pattern, the overall trend is up. If you are certain of a company then keep buying the stock when it drops. Corporate culture is the combination of values, beliefs, and behaviors demonstrated within a company. These determine how a company's employees and management interact, perform, and handle business transactions. Corporate culture is implied, not expressly defined, and develops organically over time. We feel now is a good time to invest in stalwart companies starting with their price chart.

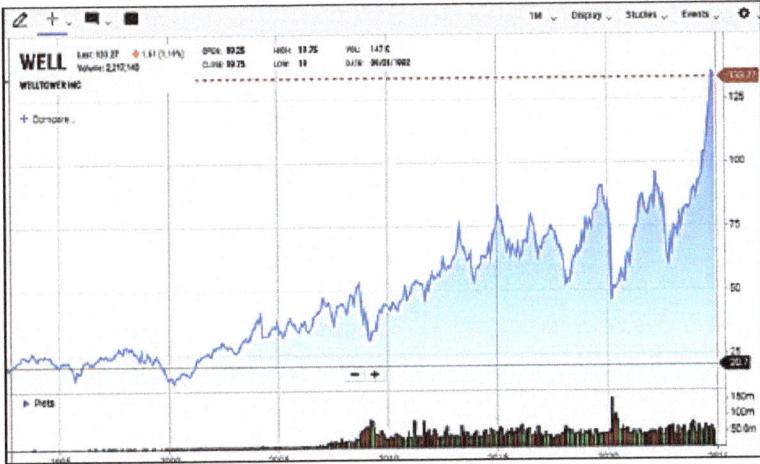

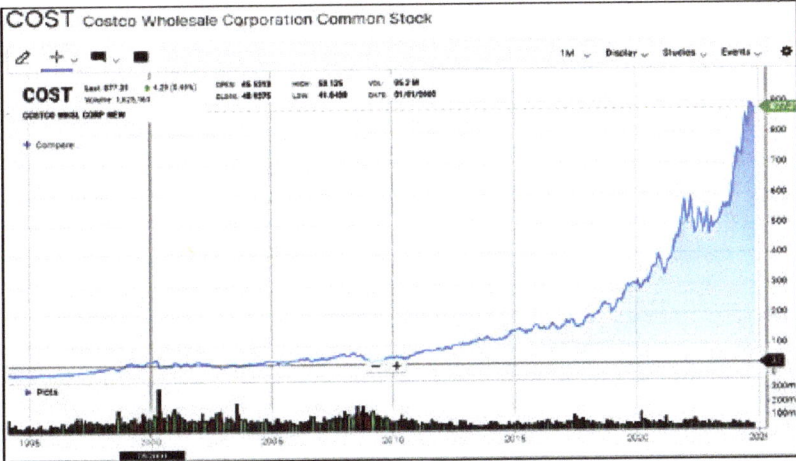

COST Costco Wholesale Corporation Common Stock

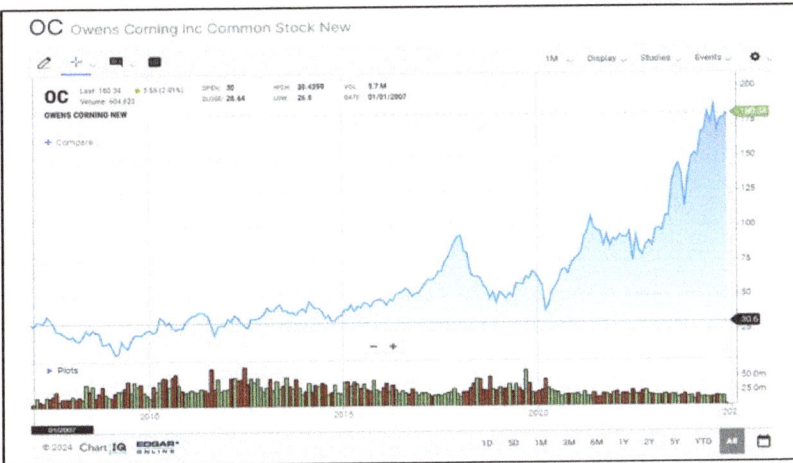

OC Owens Corning Inc Common Stock New

The Neglected Class—You

If you use one of the online brokerage accounts or, better yet, a full-service brokerage, you will often see the words "Wealth Management." Brokers want to manage your money for you, but they want you to begin with $25,000 or more. We are here to help you go from zero to $10,000 or more in small amounts added over time. We are most familiar with Merrill Lynch direct online investing and recommend them because they offer free analyst reports. But other brokers such as E*TRADE provide similar services. E*TRADE, bought by Morgan Stanley, provides brokerage reports on many stocks in various industries. We will try to keep it simple. We've been using Merrill Lynch for over forty years. But please contact others as well to see which one suits you best. Depending on whether you plan to manage your stock portfolio yourself or turn it over to someone else, there are numerous brokers available, such as Wells Fargo, Morgan Stanley, J.P. Morgan, UBS, Raymond James, Edward Jones, and others. The goal of all brokerage companies is Assets Under Management (AUM). But you want to establish your own Assets Under Your Own Management. This book is a do-it-yourself tool for investing, and we'll show you how to step-by-step. As a sidebar, we have used The Motley Fool. Looking back, that's when we discovered the magic of long-term holding. But not all their stock recommendations work out just as some of your investments will disappoint. They are not infallible. Failures are part of the landscape of investing. You must keep trying new ingredients until you find the recipes that work for you.

You likely have a retirement account managed by the company that holds your 401k. You select from the funds they offer, but someone else selects what's in those funds. This is your safe money. We suggest you continue with whatever savings you presently have. You can also create a self-directed 401k or Roth IRA based on what you learn here. Imagine all your funds—retirement, savings, pensions, IRAs, or gold coins as a bridge over a river. You need to be able to cross it safely for many years to come. Your 401k, IRA, or pension is half of a bridge being built with your money coming from one side of the river. The other half will be the portion of the bridge where you provide the finance, labor, and project management to complete. Both sides require time and attention. You must be patient. There may be floods (i.e. recessions, pandemics, etc.) that slow your progress. But care and planning will lead to success.

Bridge from the west bank of the river:	Bridge from the east bank of the river:
Your 401k, IRA or company pensions	Individual stock portfolio you will create
Composed of money market funds, mutual funds, bonds, and stock of the company you work for.	This will be the account(s) where you buy and sell individual stocks and maybe some mutual funds.
Some stocks most widely held by mutual funds:	Examples of stocks we recommend that you might hold:
Johnson & Johnson Apple Miscosoft United Healthcare Alphabet Meta Nvidia	Eli Lilly Target VISA Bank of America Comcast or Disney Progressive Insurance or Chubb Insurance

Part I
Begin at the Beginning:

The Set-Up and
Preparation for Investing

Chapter 1

Why this Book is for You:
Developing a Personal Vision
is Your First Ingredient

I found that the recipes in most - in all - the books I had were really not adequate. They didn't tell you enough... I won't do anything unless I'm told why I'm doing it. So, I felt that we needed fuller explanations so that if you followed one of those recipes, it should turn out exactly right.

—Julia Child

We do not wish to alarm you, but tomorrow you will have one less day available to shape your financial future. This is a fact, not hype. As Ann Landers used to say in her advice column, "Wake up and smell the coffee." This entire book is a call to action over the one area where you don't have to get others to agree or wait for a law to take effect—your life and your investment decisions. Never tell yourself you don't have enough money to invest, or you don't have the talent to manage your own investments. Many brokers, such as E*TRADE and Merrill Lynch Direct, require no minimum investment to open an account. We started with $100. Establish your own future to whatever extent you can. But fight for success and glory. Think of yourself as a new nation and plant your flag in an investment account with your name on it. We will provide logistics to make you successful.

No matter how long you have been investing or even if you have never invested before, you need to decide if you are happy with your investments. All of us fall into a kind of lethargy once we make an investment decision.

Investments need periodic review, but not daily, weekly or monthly changes. The investment world is in constant flux. No strategy works forever. But the change is gradual in most cases. In other cases, some companies, like pharmaceutical companies, remain forever young and continue to adapt. They have a natural pipeline and infrastructure always looking for a new drug. But the products and services most companies offer change slowly and their fortunes often remain stable. We provide examples for you to build your portfolio in the last chapter. But don't skip there until you have read most of the book.

We wish we had met someone like us when we first started investing! Of course, they were there, but we did not know who to ask. Until self-directed investing became available, everyone had to work with a broker. Brokers were not always teachers. Primarily, they were salespersons. However, the best route is to become your own source of guidance and information. Outside advice may or may not fit your investment goals. We will give you as many ideas as we can, but we always focus on investing in individual stocks. We will mention many investment tools, but we will focus on discovering and buying individual stocks over mutual funds. There are many mutual funds, and we encourage you to explore them as well.

There are roughly 8,000 stocks representing companies (both foreign and domestic). They may be small or very large. You will only need to buy and monitor a dozen stocks. Imagine a chef setting up a restaurant. She has been trained in a fundamental culinary tradition. Within that tradition she has discovered the dishes, ingredients, and spices that suit her best. That makes her cooking unique. Mutual funds are the same. They tend to specialize in areas such as health care or large cap stocks. The combinations of stocks are too many to count.

> *The stock market is like attending a professional football game and everyone in attendance chooses one side or the other. Stocks have those rooting for the shares to rise and others rooting for the stocks to loose value.*

There are many smart people investing, getting ready to invest, or getting ready to sell stocks at any given moment. On days when stocks take a tumble, as on September 3, 2024, there are a lot of sellers. There also may be several buyers. At the end of the day, every share finds a home. It's sometimes like musical chairs, but there is a seat for every stock (either someone bought at a discount, or the market maker purchased the stock, placing it in inventory). Neither you nor we can be the smartest person in the room. But long-term investors don't need to be. Sure, it hurts to lose hundreds of dollars on down days. Focus on the future not on any given day when the stock market falls or gains. You cannot be in every stock that is rising or know when to sell every stock before it falls. Keep building your portfolio until you have reached a level you want. Think of it like building a house for your family or a small cabin you can retreat to on weekends. But do not be swayed by the gyrations of the stock market either going up or down. Stay focused on finding good stocks first then worry about when to buy them.

To Own or Not To Own Individual Stocks

Most of us have been brainwashed into thinking we're not sophisticated enough to assess, buy, monitor, or re-assess the stocks of individual companies such as IBM, Exxon, Altria, Microsoft, or Apple as they are so big and complex that we, mere peasants in God's fields, don't have the ability to understand them. To some extent that's correct, so we must read the reports of several analysts. Merrill Lynch offers their own analysts' reports plus, because of rules associated with securities fraud in the industry years ago, they also must offer reports from competitors. A client at Merrill Lynch has access to Merrill reports as well as those from Morningstar and CFRA (Center for Financial Research and Analysis) which was the old Standard and Poor's research. It's not easy to find on their website, but it's there. Morgan Stanley's research is also available with an E*TRADE account. Again, they're not easy to find, but the reports are there.

First, when you purchase a mutual fund, you are buying someone else's best ideas. To be successful with that approach, you must buy several mutual funds just to get the right amount of diversification. It will cost less to buy individual stocks to get the diversification you need when starting out. If you can find an outstanding money manager such as Stanley Druckenmiller (whose fund has been closed to new investors since 2010) or Warren Buffet, then buy a mutual fund. But you might be better off looking in the mirror.

Second, we have been told that the only way to diversify is through a mutual fund. However, because many mutual funds focus on one area such as healthcare or energy, you would have to own several mutual funds to get the correct balance of diversification. No one is off the hook when diversifying their holdings. But it's not rocket science either. We recommend you buy only one stock in an industry. At the top of every Morningstar report the category of the company they are assessing is printed. For example, Albemarle Corp. (ALB) is in the Specialty Chemicals category. If you already own a stock in that classification, move on to another industry. On the other hand, if you read the report and think Albemarle is a great investment in the chemical specialty area, then we recommend you sell the one you own before buying Albemarle. There is the option of holding a second specialty chemical maker if you think that's an area that will do well for owning more than one company in one sector. Just understand what you did. We'll talk more about knowing when to break the rules later.

Third, owning stocks in individual companies is riskier than holding a mutual fund. There are two kinds of risk associated with stocks—systematic risk and idiosyncratic risk. Systematic risk comes from factors that all companies face, such as recessions, wars, and pandemics. Idiosyncratic risks are those associated with a single company. When the Deepwater Horizon rig blew up, the stock of BP (British Petroleum) was impacted but not the stocks of other oil companies. Anything can happen and does. A bank or securities firm might discover, too late, that a rogue trader bought or sold more options than she was authorized to do, and the bank's earnings took a large hit. We recommend maintaining a roughly 8-10% allocation in your portfolio with each stock you own. This, of course, applies only after you reach 10-12 stocks. Again, if you buy a big winner, it may, over time, become a larger percentage of your portfolio than you expected, but that's a good thing. See the portfolio amounts of the stocks we use as examples throughout these pages.

Investment firms sell bonds and stock for companies that they recommend. After WorldCom went bankrupt in 2002, laws were established to help investors get opinions produced by other investment firms. You, too, should practice reading more than one analyst's view of any stock you are researching. We encourage you to take every recommendation with a grain of salt. Morningstar stock reports are often available at your local library, or you can subscribe to their service. If you are willing to research a stock before you buy it, then you have the capability to be as informed as you want to be.

Fourth, our parents and grandparents owned individual stocks. They held them in some cases until they passed away and left them to other family members.

Lastly, do the richest people in America own individual stocks? You bet they do. Warren Buffet and Charlie Munger through Berkshire Hathaway only owned individual stocks or they bought the entire company as others continued to manage them. Bill Gates owns Microsoft stock although he has diversified to some extent over the years. Managers of companies own the stocks of the companies they work for and run. It's the best argument we can think of to own individual stocks. It keeps you focused and avoids the urge to jump ship when the inevitable wave hits. Owning stock in individual companies makes you think like an owner. This is not to say there are never good reasons to sell, but it will make you think twice before playing around with your portfolio. The only caveat now is that our world changes so quickly you can no longer drive a stake in the ground and say you will own any stock for your entire lifetime. When the time comes, you will likely sell a stock you have owned for a long time, either because you need the money or the company has reached a plateau. Our experience demonstrates the general rule that stocks are a good thing to own year after year. Mutual funds, because they include multiple stocks, are less volatile than individual stocks over short periods of time. But they should be held for longer as well. If you find you cannot sleep well at night, then ditch individual stocks and invest in mutual funds. Watch Peter Lynch's videos on YouTube for his insights. He says that most people did not stay in the Fidelity Magellan Fund when he ran it and missed the best gains. Whatever you decide, hold the investment as long as you can.

> It's not market timing that will benefit your portfolio. It is time in the market that keeps you from missing out on the best days. These are the days that matter most.

Our goal is for you to create an investment account and then, over time, pick one stock at a time to accumulate about ten to twelve investments. If you are starting out, it may take you ten years to develop such a portfolio because you must set aside a regular amount to invest. You likely have a lot of different demands on your finances—house, car, education, children, retirement, healthcare, pets—the list is long. To have enough liquid assets upon retirement, the average wage earner must save more than they planned to live in retirement the way they did while they were working. Even if you own a house, you can't assess its future value easily. It's better to have funds you know and manage that you can build into the size of your house's value. What we're saying is to add up what you (and a spouse) have from savings, pensions, 401k, IRA, Roth IRA and the stock account we're suggesting to equal or exceed the value of your home.

> The only rule to follow when managing your own portfolio is: Never compare what you own to what anyone else owns.

Your Financial Map

For most of us, our financial life is like a river that gets deeper and wider as time goes on. It starts as a small spring from our first job the same way rivers start naturally at their source. You must nourish it and follow it until the end of your life. Then hopefully you can divide it among your heirs, and they can enlarge their own separate streams. Think of your financial life at the end as looking like the total river basin of the Mississippi River.

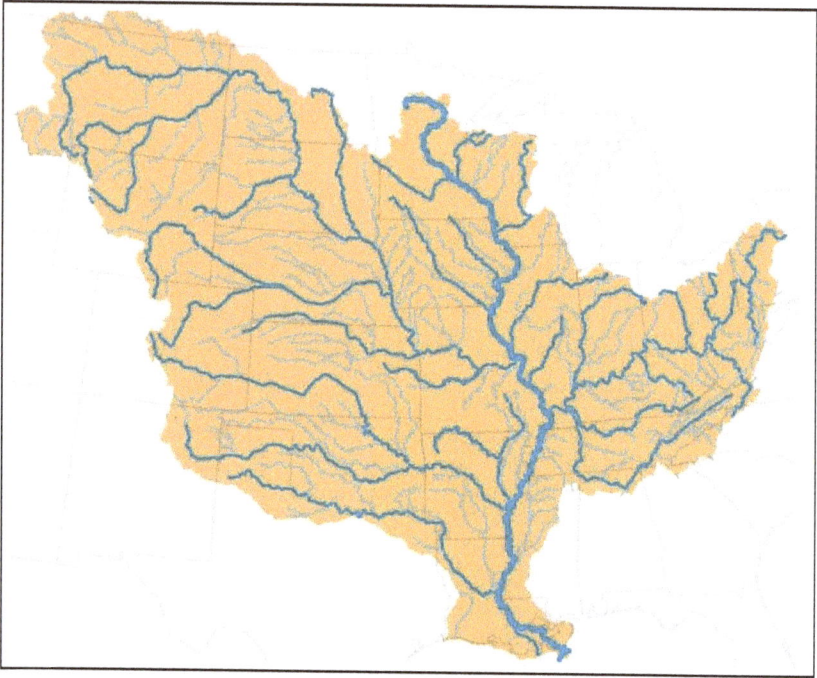

At a river's source you just step or jump across it. You may be starting with a few hundred or thousands of dollars, your initial river of wealth. But like the cities that spring up along rivers, put some aside into a reservoir for times when the river dries up or its flow is restricted for some reason. We'll discuss this more in a later chapter.

The delta of the river is your retirement or the inheritance that you will pass on to others. But your income alone will not provide enough strength to get you where you wish to be. Every river of any size starts very small at its source and increases in size as it is joined by other streams and even other rivers to add to its volume. Use your own name to give your financial river its name—the River Sam, Jennifer's River, the Elizabeth River, the River George. The first tributary will be your IRA or pension if you're lucky enough to work for a company that offers one. Many municipal workers don't have large salaries and may never have large incomes, but they receive pensions when they retire. If your company does not have a pension, it may offer an IRA. Those are your first tributaries.

You might receive an inheritance from a relative or other loved one. This income is an additional tributary that adds to your river. But you can also build your own tributaries—such as Roth IRA, Mutual Funds, and individual stocks. Match your tools to your goals. You must save as much as possible from your income to invest. Don't spend all your money. Some scholars have stated that our entire capitalist system is based on the Protestant tenet of delayed gratification that some religions espouse. Imagine you have tributaries named Savings, Bonds, Mutual Funds and finally "Portfolio." The "Portfolio" could contain stocks where each stock pays a dividend, and those would also become small tributaries. Your investments evolve over time.

Companies build their rivers of earnings the same way. Amazon started as an online book-selling company. Today, they utilize or "rent" their platform allowing other companies to sell through the Amazon "storefront" concept. They also have a huge server platform (called a data center) that serves as the "cloud" for their customers. Each business that Amazon created serves as a tributary of earnings that provides a large river of earnings in the end.

When you create your portfolio, imagine you are the Mississippi River. It's composed of many other rivers and streams. Parts of it come from the mountains in the west and part from mountains in the east. But it also receives rain from the Great Plains. If one part of the country is dry, it will receive more of its volume from other areas. Occasionally, the whole nation gets too much rain or not enough, affecting the level of the Mississippi too much in one direction or the other. This will happen to your portfolio as well. But the point we wish to make is to diversify. Imagine there is an investment that pays dividends at the headwaters of each of these streams. As they combine, the cash flow from each provides greater and greater funds over the years for you. Over decades, you will want to convert more and more of your portfolio into income producing assets. But we want to help you to create the portfolio, so you will have something to convert into income when the time comes.

We will reference the best portfolio we managed from 2009 to 2024. It's included here to show examples of what to do and what not to do. We managed this portfolio for a close friend who allowed us to use it for demonstration purposes in this book. This friend has several tributaries that make up her delta of incomes.

She has an IRA, a savings account, a pension, an account composed of stock where she worked, and another smaller investment account (which we manage as well) besides the one you will see on these pages. We're using it because it reflects principles applied over fifteen years but doesn't follow all our rules because the owner is the ultimate decision maker for our recommendations. Also, it does not show stocks sold and the money reapplied to the ones currently in the portfolio.

We did not start in 2009 thinking a book would emerge from those efforts. Otherwise, we might have saved more detailed records. But the finished product is enough, we think. It is also not the only investment our friend has.

This portfolio represents stocks acquired over the years and is more of a finished product than some of the intermediate portfolios and other "recipes" we will use for illustrations.

On May 22, 2020, our friend's E*TRADE portfolio stood at:

Symbol	Last price	Qty #	Price Pd	Day's Gain	Tot Gain	Value
AAPL	$318.89	100	$29.67	$204.00	$28,914.15	$31,889.00
AMZN	$2,436.88	10	$991.62	-$98.60	$14,436.65	$24,368.80
EQIX	$670.02	26.79	$194.38	$686.51	$12,745.00	$17,953.76
BABA	$199.70	50	$140.81	-$623.00	$2,937.25	$9,985.00
WIX	$216.21	40	$82.34	$336.00	$5,307.73	$8,608.40
DHI	$54.06	100	$35.46	$106.00	$1,852.49	$5,406.00
Total			$32,017.69	$610.91	$66,193.28	$98,210.96

On August 18, 2020, at close after withdrawing nearly $20,000 for repairs to a river house:

Symbol	Last price	Qty #	Price Pd	Day's Gain	Tot Gain	Value
AAPL	$462.25	100	$29.67	$382.00	$43,250.15	$46,225.00
AMZN	$3,312.49	10	$991.62	$1,300.80	$23,192.75	$33,124.90
BABA	$259.20	50	$140.81	$112.00	$5,912.25	$12,960.00
WIX	$286.80	40	$82.34	$164.40	$8,171.33	$11,472.00
DHI	$73.54	100	$35.46	$21.00	$3,800.49	$7,354.00
Total			$26,808.93	$1,980.20	$66,193.28	$111,217.92

She sold Equinix and had some other cash. These numbers are actual, untampered with. The portfolio soared that summer. She also has a smaller portfolio of stocks with Merrill Lynch. The combined portfolios contain about ten stocks.

Rules for Your Portfolio

1. Aim to own ten to twelve stocks. It's enough to keep track of for most of us. Our example portfolio used to contain more stocks, but as the owner needed money, she sold smaller holdings or those that lost money. Plus, she has another account with five additional stocks.

2. Each stock should be in an industry or business different from all the others. (See our Pantry Stock Chapter 13 for the broad sectors.) Spread your purchases among the various sectors. Diversification is key. But sometimes you will discover what Peter Lynch once said, "The best stock to buy may be the one you already own."

3. If one stock reaches more than ten percent of the portfolio, sell some of it and buy an additional stock in another industry. But if the stock is just too good to sell, allow it to grow into a larger percentage of the portfolio. See Apple in our friend's portfolio examples throughout the book.

4. Don't sell stocks short. [i.e. borrowing a stock you do not own and selling it in the hopes it will decline in value so that you can buy it back cheaper.] It's a job for professionals and not for the average investor.

5. Read analysts' reports on the companies you own and follow quarterly earnings reports. There is homework required when you buy and sell your own stocks (Jim Cramer's rule).

6. Don't fret over short-term price swings in your stocks. They go up and they go down like the weather. If a stock falters badly, you will know it.

7. Decide how much risk you're willing to accept with any given stock.

8. Give your stocks at least three years before you sell them. More on this later.

9. Be comfortable with your decisions. If owning a stock or even being in the stock market for a few months makes you uneasy, sell the stock or the portfolio and put the money into a money market fund. Do not risk your sleep or, worse yet, your health.

10. Be proud of what you own. Think of your stocks as players on a team you manage or students who get report cards every quarter. Celebrate when things work out.

11. Don't brag but give yourself a pat on the shoulder. Know that they are still working hard when things don't turn out well sometimes. It gets better for most companies most of the time.

Stocks Are Ingredients in Your Recipe for Success

Stocks are like the ingredients in the grocery store with literally thousands of cans and packages of varying sizes. You don't buy twelve jars of mayo at one time. If you want to make a sandwich, you buy one jar of mayo, a head of lettuce, tomatoes, bread, meat, cheese, pickles, chips, and napkins. That's a recipe for a sandwich portfolio. A similar stock portfolio might include a bank, a pharmaceutical company, an entertainment company, an infrastructure company, a new technology company, and a food company.

In 2020, we made a list of stocks we could have bought from recommendations we found. This exercise turned out to be an eye-opening revelation when we reviewed them in 2024. Some went down; some went up. We did not own any of these stocks. It was a research portfolio only. But some that did not go up may be better buys now. We learned that if you don't "bet the farm" on one stock, you will be all right. Create your own "pretend" portfolio to see if you are cooking effectively. Make lists of potential companies you read about and examine them over time. We made this list before we discovered the elements that indicate a good stock for the long term that we cover in this book. We got about half of them right. We didn't know in 2020 what we now know in 2024.

1. Bank United (BKU) - Industry: Regional Banks
2. Jazz Pharmaceuticals (JAZZ) - Industry: Biotechnology
3. Surgery Partners (SGRY) - Industry: Medical Specialty
4. SYNNEX (SNX) - Industry: Information Technology
5. Skyworks Solutions (SWKS) - Industry: Semiconductors
6. Tractor Supply Company (TSCO) - Industry: Specialty Retail
7. Lincoln National (LNC) - Industry: Insurance and Financial Services
8. Fox Factory Holding (FOXF) - Industry: Recreational Vehicles
9. CrowdStrike Holdings (CRWD) - Industry: Software—Infrastructure
10. Jabil Inc. (JBL) - Electronic Components

Comparing the prices of these stocks in 2024 to what they were in 2020 led us to the conclusions you will read here. Note: what we selected in 2020 would not have been the best choices by 2024. We learned from our mistakes as you will. If we had bought all these stocks, we would likely have sold those that went down over time.

Make a list of ten to twelve stocks you like now, pretend you own them, and create your first watchlist. See which ones go up. Delete the worst performers after several months and keep the rest. It will always be a mixed bag of gains and losses. But you can hold those that might become your foundation stocks.

An old Wall Street adgage that retains its relevance:
Cut your losses. Let your winners run.

Not all the above are small capitalization stocks. Those that are mid-cap were selected because they are smaller than the huge companies in their industry. We would argue they are relatively smaller cap than the industry names you are more familiar with. Also, we don't include any direct investments in many foreign companies. Jazz Pharmaceuticals is headquartered in Ireland, but most of its research and sales take place in the United States. Since 2020, some have declined dramatically while others have continually gone up in price. The point is that you don't have to pick all winners and things may still be fine. Go back five years to these stocks on *Finance.Yahoo.com* to see for yourself. For centuries, farmers have planted various crops and specialized in the ones that grew the most. When this country was settled along the James River in Virginia, the colonists failed to sustain themselves or bring in money. They finally planted tobacco which became the sustaining crop that ultimately allowed the colony to flourish. A few stocks will sustain your investment. Some will seem to be dead but still have life.

Another Way to View Your Portfolio Is to Envision It As a Symphony Orchestra

Assume you are the conductor. You have a standard arrangement but sometimes you must add an instrument because a piece requires a tenor bassoon or some other instrument not normally a part of the orchestra. Imagine you are creating a portfolio. Microsoft and Apple are like first or second violins, so there are more shares of those than any other section. Cellos

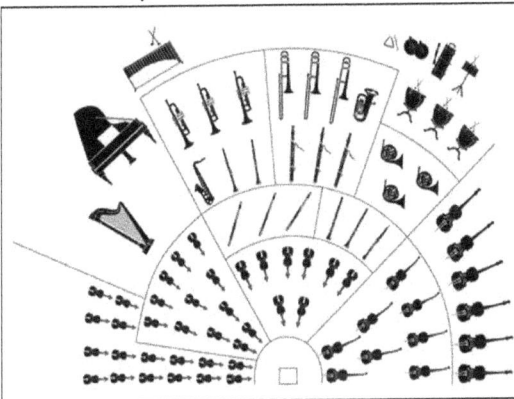

represent utilities in your portfolio. Violas are software stocks or financial stocks. Each stock contributes to the overall performance of your portfolio. From time to time, a stock (like an instrument) gets a solo part and performs more prominently.

First Things First

First, before you invest, you want to work in a stable job (as much as is possible in this world) in a stable industry or career. If you have established yourself as a valuable, trusted employee, then stay in your job. Don't look around. The most successful investors come out of the ranks of those with stable, long-term employment. That way you don't have to panic when (not if) the stock market goes down. We will repeat this fact more than once—when the market goes down you must stay the course. Since the stock market is based on economic, financial, political, and unexpected events that are out of anyone's control, it will decline from time to time. It has never failed to come back. But human nature and fear cause it to swing wildly at times. Witness the most recent gyrations during the Coronavirus (COVID-19) of 2020. Some of the movement was justified. People predicted they would need some cash. But, when you add panic selling, money managers protecting their performances, and those who were looking for opportunities to short the market, you get the major lows of March 2020.

Second, own a house or other real estate that is not tied to the stock market. A house typically proves to be the single best investment an individual can make. In your early years, with a mortgage, the principal (even if small) acts like a savings account. Plus, houses increase in value at least at the same rate as inflation. Because the population continues to grow, demand for your house increases. In Central Virginia, many newcomers had sold houses they owned for many years while they worked for the government and lived in metropolitan Washington, D.C. Back in the 1950s and sixties, many small houses were built in Chevy Chase and Silver Spring, Maryland that soared in value. Likewise, small houses in Alexandria and Falls Church, Virginia increased in value approximately fivefold over most people's careers. As Peter Lynch said in his famous book, *One Up on Wall Street*, "A house is entirely rigged in the homeowner's favor." His book is filled with nuggets of wisdom and insights. Houses generally are owned for many years. While you won't move into one of your stocks, aim for stock ownership as if you were buying the whole company. Someone asked Warren Buffet what the timeframe was that he used for stocks. His reply was "forever."

We will show in the following examples that stocks need to be given time to grow. Imagine they are children. Their initial timeframe will be five years before they start school. Then perhaps another twelve years until they get through high school. After twenty years you can release/sell them if you want. We all know of old relatives who left behind beautiful old stock certificates they had received forty or more years earlier with names like Standard Oil of New Jersey or Coca Cola Company. Do not expect your stocks to provide a quick fortune. Get rich slowly. Buy a house first. Enjoy it, live in it, and keep it in good repair. Then you'll be ready to buy stocks.

Third, maintain a savings account of six months of living expenses. You can cheat on this requirement by keeping part of that cash in the investment account you will need for purchasing stocks. More on that later. The Coronavirus, so wildly unexpected, showed that this kind of insurance policy, while rarely needed, comes in handy when the unexpected occurs. Americans are woefully deficient when it comes to saving.

Fourth, review what your near-term financial needs are before committing money to stocks. For example, will you need to pay tuition for a child going to college; assist a parent or relative with living expenses; renovate the kitchen or add a room onto your home; or buy a new car soon? Stocks are for sale every single business day. They will be there when you are ready. Don't rush this. Stocks are waiting for you. The stock market is like going to a dance where partners two to three deep are along every wall. Invest when you comfortably have the money available.

> *If you have trouble managing a 20% loss in the stock market, you shouldn't be trading in stocks.*
> **- John Dogle, founder of the Vanguard Funds**

Last, ask yourself who you are. The stock market is a terrible place to find out what your tolerance for risk is or your suitability to research stocks and ability to hold them. Imagine how you will react the first time you lose money. There are internet tools where you can create imaginary portfolios and watch them over time. But act as if it were your real money and see how it feels. It's like driving a car before you purchase it. Can you easily see around you? Are the controls easy to read? How much maintenance does it require? Stocks generally go up over long periods of time but can have unpredictable near-term swings. If you hold ten stocks, one of them can come down with a severe illness. Look what happened to Boeing in 2019 and then in 2020.

Its reputation was destroyed by the 737 MAX crashes, and before that could be resolved a great proportion of air traffic demand was destroyed by the Coronavirus. Those events showed that Boeing was a broken corporation. Up to some point, there were detailed procedures in place for building and certifying an aircraft for operation. An investor cannot see inside a company she owns for clues.

Boeing stock lost almost 75% of its value at the pit of the pandemic. Look at its chart and imagine you bought it for $440 on February 25, 2019. Would you have sold out on March 16, 2020, when it hit $95? We tell ourselves we would have seen the stock falling and sold way before it got so low. Well, my friend, at the end of each day someone or some institution owns all the stock of every company. These things happen so fast sometimes that you can't get out of the way soon enough. It would have been better to have owned ten shares of Boeing at its height and bought ten more at its low or near there and wait it out. Remember you have a house to live in and six months of savings or more to tide you over. Never expect stocks to provide quick money.

Now in 2024, with the installation of Kelly Ortberg as CEO, a new phase may be starting. Ortberg is credited with building Rockwell Collins into a major aerospace supplier with an outstanding culture of engineering expertise. Rockwell Collins was what Boeing used to be. Naturally, he made a good fit for Boeing. It will take a very long time for Boeing to re-establish the place it held prior to its current troubles. But a major change such as this could make Boeing a promising investment. Do not ask yourself if a stock is a good investment today. Ask yourself if it will still be a good investment in five years.

What To Expect

We anticipate it will take you six years to reach $10,000. This target is full of assumptions, but they are not wild assumptions. We are developing a portfolio along with you and shall see if we can duplicate these results closely. Your total investment will be $7,200 ($1,200 / year).

The above example is based on several assumptions. We are not making any allowance for a severe fall in the market. We assume that you can make regular deposits each month. We assume your portfolio will gain 7% *on average* each year through share price appreciation, and perhaps some dividends, with the usual caveat that there is always a risk of losing money when investing in the stock market. We would rather under-promise and over-deliver than the other way around. We want to predict average returns and be surprised.

	Begin Bal	Cash in	Dividends	Price Rise	Total End of Year
Year One	$0.00	$100 x 12	$ 40.00	$84.00	$1,324.00
Year Two	$1,384.00	$1,200.00	$ 50.00	$190.00	$2,764.00
Year Three	$2,874.00	$1,200.00	$ 60.00	$301.00	$4,325.00
Year Four	$4,325.00	$1,200.00	$ 80.00	$420.00	$6,025.00
Year Five	$6,025.00	$1,200.00	$100.00	$549.00	$7,874.00
Year Six	$7,874.00	$1,200.00	$130.00	$687.00	$9,891.00

This Happens Every Single Day

If you open *Finance.Yahoo.com* each day, you will see headlines about a company making decisions. Some of the decisions are good ones. Some of the decisions don't work out as they expected. Even on days the stock market is closed, someone is creating content that will predict the rise or fall of a stock. No one ever says, "they will do what they did yesterday and every day going forward." Who wants to hear that? You do. You don't want a stock you own to be constantly in the news. Instead, you want stocks like Berkshire Hathaway owns such as Coca-Cola or American Express. No one reads or writes about businesses staying the same, but it's remarkable how many consistent earners of small amounts have accumulated wealth. Look for the kind of company in which you would buy stock for your mother. Then buy it for yourself.

If you are ready to invest based on your self-assessment, then let's get started.

Chapter 2

The Starting Gate

No one remembers what you started.
—unknown

Your Goal

Long ago, a friend advised me to "play your game; don't play their game" since there is so much distracting noise. If you decide to take charge of some or all of your own investments, you will have a better chance of designing and implementing the results you want. You do not have to invest in the way others design your path.

We will give you specific "recipes" with specific stocks that you can buy and hold if you agree with our recommendations. Better yet, we'll show you how to acquire and monitor information that will better suit your unique personality and situation. Invest in the way you design it; don't invest in the way others design it for you.

Step Zero

Set up an investment account with a brokerage or a mutual fund company. Nowadays, most mutual fund companies offer the option of buying and selling individual stocks. Here are some of our favorites:

- Merrill Lynch (Bank of America)

- T. Rowe Price (known for mutual funds but can also serve as a broker)

- E*TRADE

- Vanguard

Some of these require minimum investments for various kinds of accounts. Mutual funds require minimums. You can research various investments on their sites. E*TRADE currently relies on the research of its parent company, Morgan Stanley. Some mutual funds allow you to set up your account with no money if you set up automatic deductions from your bank with a minimum going into a mutual fund.

Think of yourself as a tithe. Add your name to the list of institutions you tithe to. If you don't tithe to anything outside of your family, then still put yourself first. It doesn't have to be ten percent. It can be ten dollars. But set up a fixed amount that you will save monthly to help you build your investments. If you say you cannot afford to save money to buy stocks, then you can stop right here and give this book to someone who might benefit from using it. We cannot have everything we want instantly. The concept of deferred gratification helped Western civilization establish the economic foundations of capitalism centuries ago. There can be no progress for the average person without some degree of methodical saving. Save as much as you can. Stretch yourself. Grow your wealth step-by-step. But "get rich slow."

> *Don't assess your gains and losses in your first year if you can help it. Small and under-diversified portfolios are more volatile. Give your stocks time to grow and develop. Plus, owning stocks takes some getting used to.*

Our pastor once gave a sermon on change. He said there were three steps to making a change: fix in your mind the change you want to make, announce the change to your family and friends, and finally, expect a miracle. Going from looking for instructions and suggestions from others to doing it for yourself is a big change. Don't discount how big a challenge it is to invest based on your own reasoning.

America is at work every day. New ideas and new ways of promoting and providing goods and services happen somewhere every minute of the day. If you made a map of the United States and put icons for similar industries across the map, it would show clusters of industries in primary locations. We are a nation of factories, shops, stores, mines, fields, and forests. Commerce, and hence economic advances, spring up everywhere. We are a nation of doers. Here is your opportunity to participate in the process to your advantage.

Mutual Funds

Mutual funds equate to dining at a restaurant. They might be local, regional, national or even international. Most strive to have a variety of separate funds. There are many excellent "chains" such as T. Rowe Price, Vanguard, Fidelity, American Funds and others. The top ten mutual fund companies control over fifty percent of all the money invested in mutual funds. It's a good place to start, but you don't have to start here. You can set up your own self-directed investment account instead. Mutual funds can be a side-dish beside the portfolio you establish.

The reason to understand individual stocks is because mutual fund managers do the same thing. We're going to show you how to create a portfolio of stocks. Mutual fund managers comb through individual stocks, like you will, to pick the ones that will help them outperform their peers. Frequently, however, mutual funds focus on a select area such as precious metals, healthcare, energy, transportation, and so on. This means they are reviewing a subset of the wide universe you can pick from. You will be at an advantage selecting mutual funds, when the time comes, by knowing the names of companies that you will recognize in the lists of top holdings of mutual funds. These names are easily found by entering the five-letter symbol of the mutual fund you're interested in and viewing their top ten holdings. It's a view to the way a mutual fund manager sees the investment arena. Even if you never buy an individual stock, you will gain insight by knowing more about individual companies.

Mutual funds are a fine place to invest. Mutual fund companies buy individual stocks, so it makes sense that you know the companies your mutual fund is buying. Since their management changes, you must periodically review your holdings. They save you time. If researching is not for you, then take this path. It saves you time and your portfolio will not be as volatile as the one you may design.

Lastly, some mutual funds specialize in small-cap, mid-cap, or large-cap stocks. In these cases, they find the best companies based on capitalizing the company first. The larger the company size, the more "liquid" its stock. The market capitalization of any company is easily found on *Finance.Yahoo.com* by putting in the symbol and the market cap that can be found at the top of the right column below the chart. Faster growing companies usually have smaller market caps.

Whichever way you invest, your efforts at obtaining knowledge of individual stocks will not be wasted. Depending on how much money you can invest, you may even have a mix of mutual funds and individual stocks. Our view is that you are going to build a mutual fund of your own, such as Sally's Small-cap Mutual fund, Bob's Big-cap Fund, Jenny's Mid-cap Fund.

The Major Drawback of Mutual Funds

Mutual funds invest not only in various stocks but may also include many other asset types such as bonds and even other mutual funds to reach their goals. However, the Investment Company Act of 1940 limits how much a diversified fund can invest in any single stock. Under this act, there are rules and oversight to mitigate risk for investors. Companies such as Vanguard and Fidelity also have guidelines that their mutual funds must follow. Look for these guidelines as you become more sophisticated in investing. If a stock is a real winner, a mutual fund will have to sell off a portion to maintain the maximum percentage allowed to be invested in a single stock.

In the case of our friend's portfolio, if her portfolio were a mutual fund then she would have to sell off shares of Apple as it continued to rise in price from 2009 to 2024, and she would not have been able to hold as much Amazon stock as she owned. This, to us, is another reason to manage your own portfolio. You control how much concentration you have in a single sector or stock. But do not ignore the experience of past generations that created these rules. Each mutual fund company, such as T. Rowe Price, Fidelity and all the others, have guidelines their managers must follow. In the summer of 2020 as we began this book, mutual fund managers were lagging the "market" because they could not hold concentrations such as the ones in the portfolio snapshots we show. Hedge funds and others continuously bid up the stock prices of Apple, Microsoft, Netflix, Amazon, and Alphabet, as examples. Other studies show that over time mutual funds lag the S&P 500 Index not because the managers are incompetent but because they must work at a disadvantage with one hand tied behind their backs. Remember the three-legged races from your childhood? Mutual fund managers have one leg tied to numerous rules that mean they might lag the market. Finally, many mutual funds require an initial investment of $2,500 or more. The good news is that as the market has risen so have all the mutual funds.

A big advantage you have regarding mutual funds is you do not have to compare your performance to any benchmarks. Often a superior company's price will lag not only the market but its peers as well. Money managers can't stick with some companies for too long. You, as your own manager, can hold a stock until its value reaches a point where the price of the stock reflects what you think the company is worth. Stocks of oil-related industries have been "crushed" in the last five years due to exogenous factors—over production by Saudi Arabia, Russia and other foreign producers, and self-imposed, domestic overproduction. If the world returns to "normal," defined as pre-pandemic operations, oil-related stocks may rise. But this can take a long time. But recall what John Maynard Keynes said, "The market can stay irrational longer than you can stay solvent." The flexibility of the individual investor makes holding individual stocks a winning long-term strategy.

Finally, wherever you are in the market cycle or your own personal investing journey, remember to remain optimistic. You will always be your own worst critic. The first stock you buy will either go down or up based on what the market does. It may languish for what becomes a tortuous interval after you buy it. Think of it as one of your children studying a foreign language for the first time. Give it time to prove you right. Stock prices obey a natural cycle where sales must rise first before earnings show, and this process can take numerous quarters. For example, if you purchase a drug stock, you can expect approvals, launches, sales campaigns, and acceptance by doctors and patients to take a long time. But with patience, you can win and be validated in your purchase in the long run.

Our friend is a case in point. Some stocks we advised her to sell too soon. After the initial 7-for-1 split of the original twenty-five shares of Apple occurred, the stock gradually began to rise and become a larger part of her portfolio. We suggested that she sell gradually seventy-five shares and diversify her portfolio but keep the remaining 100 shares. If she had kept the entire 175 shares at the time of the next split, her holdings would have equaled approximately $87,500 instead of $50,000 in 2020. But she might not have owned some other stocks that did well. You constantly must weigh how much to allocate and not second-guess yourself every time a stock you sell continues to rise. The market overall will rise for every stock for every investor given patience and perseverance.

Your First Purchases

Suppose you have decided to pull money out of savings and open a brokerage account to buy some stock. What should you buy? Buy the stock of a product you purchase as a consumer or homeowner. There is a list of ideas based on things we currently buy on the following page.

Why start with these or similar ones? First, they are often more stable than others because they have a solid base of customers. Second, it's like paying yourself as the stocks gain. But it's not a one-time purchase (but it might be). Continue to invest in the stock of any that goes up. But just select two or three from this list. These will be your cornerstone or foundation stocks. Look at the products you use and research who makes them. You may be familiar with local companies such as your bank, the manufacturer of your car, who built your home, and your insurance provider. Invest in your backyard first.

Company Name	What We Use of Theirs	Amount to Invest
Dominion Power (Central VA power company) or your local power provider. Pays a dividend	Electricity—Monthly power bill	Up to $500 initially
Kroger or another grocer you use	Groceries and Gasoline	$100+ initially then more as often as you can
Comcast, Netflix, Disney	Local Cable and Internet provider, or streaming service	$100+ then more, as you can
Progressive Insurance or the one you use for car or home	Auto Insurance	$100+ then more, as you can
United Health Care or other	Health Insurance	$100+ then more, as you can

Build Your Avenue of Dreams

In a nutshell, what this book shows is how to build a personal avenue of dreams. First, we suggest you do research to find excellent companies with good prospects. Second, open an investment account and regularly fund it. Next, regularly purchase a small amount of stock, and continue to add funds to your account. Then purchase a second stock or all shares to the first stock you originally purchased. Your account is like a Monopoly board indicating your partial ownership of a company with factories, software companies, and stores. You will go around and around your avenue of dreams, adding new stock or new shares to your holdings every year as you see fit.

Chapter 3

Preparing to Invest

Setting up Your Kitchen or Workroom

This is my invariable advice to people: Learn how to cook — try new recipes, learn from your mistakes, be fearless and above all have fun!
—Julia Child

Make your place of stock research as permanent as you can. Everyone uses iPads and laptops more now than desktops. But if you do your work from different locations—coffee shops, sofa, standing desk, park bench—you lose the sense of a home place where you come to think or plan. Writers say if you show up in the same place at the same time every day, your muse will appear and guide you. Do not worry about what others do, think, or say about your space because you want to also learn not to act based on what others do, think, or say. Know that this is the place where can merge peace and mind to produce results.

Your stock research space should have the things you need, such as a calculator, this book, *Forbes* magazine, books by or about Peter Lynch or Warren Buffett, plus other investing aids. In our offices, we keep helpful books close by.

We recommend you maintain a thumb drive backup even if you back up to the cloud or somewhere else. This way when you absolutely must work somewhere else, you can access all your saved files.

Each day, scroll down the news stories on *Finance.Yahoo.com* or some other site. Yahoo lists recommendations from various brokers and analysts every day. Read some of them. If one sounds particularly helpful, highlight it, and save it to a word file for the future. Often, this site will mention a book by someone like John C. Bogle, founder of the Vanguard Funds, who wrote several books. Read one of them. If you don't have time, you can listen to his interviews on YouTube. Peter Lynch also offers YouTube videos. Bogle was a strong believer that it's not worth the effort (and it's too difficult) to beat the market, so invest in index funds and stay the course. We agree with staying the course, but we also think you will become a better investor by buying individual stocks that you have researched yourself.

There are many important basic investment books to own, read, and reread. *A Random Walk down Wall Street* by Burton G. Malkiel has stood the test of time. He is also a believer in index funds because, as the title of his book suggests, too many variables affect stock prices, and you cannot predict them. Many authors use the example of looking at a winning mutual fund one year and noting that it does not usually beat the market the next year. That is not a surprise, is it? But some mutual fund managers do beat the market over a long period of time without being able to outperform on cue every single year.

The saying goes:

When you plant English ivy - the first year it sleeps, the second year it creeps, and the third year it leaps.

Stocks often act the same way.

A manager who achieved outstanding results was Peter Lynch who ran the Fidelity Magellan Fund for many years. His book, *One Up on Wall Street*, is an entertaining and enlightening read. He advocates looking in your own backyard for hidden treasures. Here in Central Virginia where we live, there have been many excellent companies that have made people in the area significant money. Currently, excellent companies within fifty miles of us that have done well and would make suitable investments for years to come (in no particular order):

1. Markel Corporation (MKL)
2. Altria Corporation (MO)

3.   CarMax (KMX)

4.   C&F Financial (CFFI)

5.   One of the spinoffs from Ethyl Corporation:
- Albemarle Corporation
- NewMarket Corporation
- Tredegar Corporation

During the second half of the twentieth century, numerous investors became millionaires from their holdings in Ethyl Corporation and subsequent spinoffs. The Gottwald family have been major benefactors in the Richmond, Virginia area. The point is to look closely at companies with a presence or headquarters near where you live.

Another interesting book that may help your investing is *Blink: The Power of Thinking Without Thinking* by Malcolm Gladwell. There is a phenomenon that takes place in the brain where it can utilize simultaneously ten, fifteen, or twenty different observations to make a quick assessment of value. It is most easily seen when an appraiser on *Antiques Roadshow* recognizes a piece brought in by a person who has little knowledge about their "treasure." The appraiser interviews the visitor about what they know about the object. The appraiser takes that information and quickly combines it with the knowledge he or she has acquired about similar objects to put a value on it. The appraiser then gives them a "conservative" value of the piece. Interestingly, on some repeat shows, the program displays the current value of the object from an appraisal ten or more years before. Many of the objects declined in value because the "market" for those objects is not as hot as it was when the first appraisal took place. Some objects, especially artwork and objects made with precious metals or gems have risen in value. There is a similarity with stocks you may see looking at historical price charts. Michael O'Mahony says of this book:

> *How many companies have you looked at before conducting any serious due diligence, and just had a gut feeling about them? How many of these gut feelings turned out to be right? 'Blink' goes about to explain this phenomenon.*

> *While I'll leave the explanations of "thin slicing" and "the adaptive unconscious" to Gladwell himself, what 'Blink' does is examine closely the power of instincts, hunches, and those aforementioned gut feelings. Through his eye-opening case studies and what must have been a mountain of background research, he succeeds in informing us of the power of human judgment, as well as its pitfalls. It's a fascinating book that makes the reader examine their own decision-making process.*

Gladwell states that the phenomenon is not magic but a process anyone can develop from reading and combining their experiences to focus on, in our case, a stock, and know very quickly if it's a suitable investment for themselves or not.

> *The internet and other media outlets continuously highlight companies when they have great good fortune, explosive earnings, or unexpected declines in the stock price. Every day they print lists of the most active stocks, those that rose most, and those that declined the most. One day, one of your stocks may appear on these lists. Look past whatever spotlight a stock of yours appears in. Keep your eyes on the long-term activities of the company whose stock you own.*

Another way to acquire knowledge and insights quickly and without an enormous cost is to subscribe to *Forbes* magazine or free investment advice on *Finance.yahoo.com*. *Forbes* articles offer insights into companies not easily found elsewhere. Back in the 1980s a writer in *Forbes* said that contrary to popular beliefs of the time, the scientists at Pfizer (PFE) were not asleep. From that point on, Pfizer developed new drugs and purchased many other pharmaceutical companies to become the powerhouse it is now. But the stock of the company has had its ups and downs over the last thirty years. When you break down a stock into its components, it will always be a game of inches.

Finally, read one of Jim Cramer's books, but only after you are well-grounded in the stocks you own. His insights will establish the framework that shows the big picture of how stocks function in the investment environment.

When chefs buy a new restaurant or go to work at one, they must set up their kitchens to reflect the way they work. They make sure the tools they are used to working with are present and in top condition. They arrange their frequently used pots and pans close to their workstations.

How you organize your files is distinctive, so we will not presume offering any better suggestions. We just want to emphasize keeping files of all the stocks you consider. You will want them organized like farmers' fields perhaps. There will be cold frames with sprouts (your watchlist), early plantings (stocks you're waiting to buy or switch into), crops in their growth phase (the ones you own in your portfolio), and those that are ready to be harvested. Some stocks you will hold for a long time, perhaps a decade or more. Someday, you will see a price aberration too good to ignore and you will swoop down and purchase it and sell it again in a few days for a small but certain profit. This happened for us among oil stocks because the market for oil has experienced incredible gyrations. But these oil stocks are tricky and sometimes don't work out the way you expect, so we do not recommend this strategy.

It is exciting to be a chef in the stock-market kitchen. Like all cooks, you will learn and experiment. There will be dishes that you don't get right, but you will also experience extraordinary cuisine when you use the best ingredients and get the recipe right. Be prepared to wipe your hands on your apron sometimes, turn back around to the stove, and start again. Chefs, to be able to achieve their best results, must cook in the kitchen. They may use an outdoor grill from time to time, but most cooks' best results occur in their main kitchens. After preparing a dish, a chef either declares it ready to be delivered to the table and starts on the next dish or else turns back to the stove to prepare a different dish. Either way there is always another dish to be cooked.

What Not To Do When Studying Stocks

It is human nature to compare your portfolio, whatever its size, to the major indices at the end of the day. We do this too. Usually, your return is less than the S&P 500 on any given day. The composition of the index is important if you use it to compare how you are doing.

Investopedia.com explains how it works:

> *Calculating the individual market weights shows how the underlying stocks affect the index. The individual market weights are calculated by dividing the free-float market capitalization of a company in the index by the total market capitalization of the index. As of January 2019, the S&P 500 total market cap was approximately $23 trillion. [Today, in January 2025 the market capitalization is $50 trillion.] The market cap of Apple is roughly 3% market weight. Overall, the larger the market weight of a company, the more impact each 1% change in a stock's price will have on the index.*

Therefore, the largest companies dominate the index.

The following data comes from the website for *thebalance.com*. Here are the weights of each market sector in the S&P (Standard and Poor) as of August 31, 2020:

Sectors	10 Largest Components of the S&P
• Information Technology: 27.5% • Health Care: 14.6% • Consumer Discretionary: 11.2% • Communication Services: 10.9% • Financials: 9.9% • Industrials: 7.9% • Consumer Staples: 7.0% • Utilities: 3.1% • Real Estate: 2.8% • Materials: 2.6% • Energy: 2.5%	1. Apple Inc. 2. Microsoft Corp. 3. Amazon.com Inc. 4. Facebook Inc. A 5. Alphabet Inc. A (GOOGL)* 6. Alphabet Inc. C (GOOG)* 7. Johnson & Johnson 8. Berkshire Hathaway B 9. Procter & Gamble 10. Visa Inc. *Alphabet is only one company but has two classes of voting shares so listed twice.

The following data came from *Investopedia.com*. Here are the weights of each market sector in the S&P (Standard and Poor) as of August 1, 2024:

Sectors	10 Largest Components of the S&P
• Information Technology: 28.3% • Healthcare: 13.2% • Financials: 12.5% • Consumer Discretionary: 10.6% • Communication Services: 8.8% • Industrials: 8.4% • Consumer Staples: 6.6% • Energy: 4.4% • Materials: 2.5% • Real Estate: 2.4% • Utilities: 2.4%	1. Apple (AAPL): 7.05% 2. Microsoft (MSFT): 6.54% 3. Amazon (AMZN): 3.24% 4. NVIDIA (NVDA): 2.79% 5. Alphabet Class A (GOOGL): 2.13% 6. Tesla (TSLA): 1.95% 7. Alphabet Class C (GOOG): 1.83% 8. Berkshire Hathaway (BRK.B): 1.83% 9. Meta (META), Class A: 1.81% 10. UnitedHealth Group (UNH): 1.28%

As you research and study stocks, you must create mental distance from the sources that established your belief in a stock's story. Opinions and re-evaluations by analysts take place frequently. It should take a lot to shake your opinions about the stocks you hold. Warren Buffett and Morningstar both evaluate companies by assessing whether they have developed a moat around their business. The term "economic moat," popularized by Warren Buffett, refers to a company's ability to maintain competitive advantages over its competitors to protect its long-term profits and market share from competing firms.

You will need a mental moat around your research and the level of your commitment to a specific company because there is no consensus on the future price of any given stock. When you examine the history of a company's stock price, you will see extreme fluctuations. Stock prices fluctuate during recessions, market sell-offs, and many other internal and competitive events that can cause them to rise or fall.

Never compare your portfolio to one of the big averages. What you own is too much of a subset to tell you anything useful about your choices. Indexes are carefully construstructed and it's impossble to align your stocks in any manner to match an index. It is always just a concidence.

Also, if you are a customer of one of the big investment banks such as Merrill Lynch, from time to time, the analyst for a stock you bought leaves, and a new one takes over that responsibility. The new analyst probably has a different opinion about stocks you might own. So, you must do a reassessment based on the new information. Even the analysts you rely on may change their opinions of a stock.

It's okay for you to change your mind on a stock you hold, but don't be too easily swayed. Know yourself, know your goals, and know your holdings.

What To Know about the Cycles Companies Encounter

The Wheel of Retailing

Prof. Malcolm Perrine McNair proposed this theory in 1931. He specialized in the evolution of retailing, where a retail organization starts up by providing low prices, basic product features, and minimal services with a thin profit margin. Slowly the brand evolves to offer a wider range of products, higher prices, better services, and additional facilities at a considerable profit margin.

The wheel of retailing refers to a hypothesis, though we can think of many companies that fit this profile, which depicts the life cycle of a retail organization. It starts as a discount retail business to attract price-sensitive consumers and then gradually converts into a luxury-brand store or department store to cater to high-end consumers. It can be visualized as phases over the lifespan of the business. It is simple to understand theory, and many examples support the idea.

There are numerous examples of retailers that reflect this model. Here in Central Virginia Sydney and Frances Lewis founded Best Products in 1957. They sold merchandise with a well-made catalog. Thus began the "catalog showroom" concept they invented. The chain grew and expanded across the

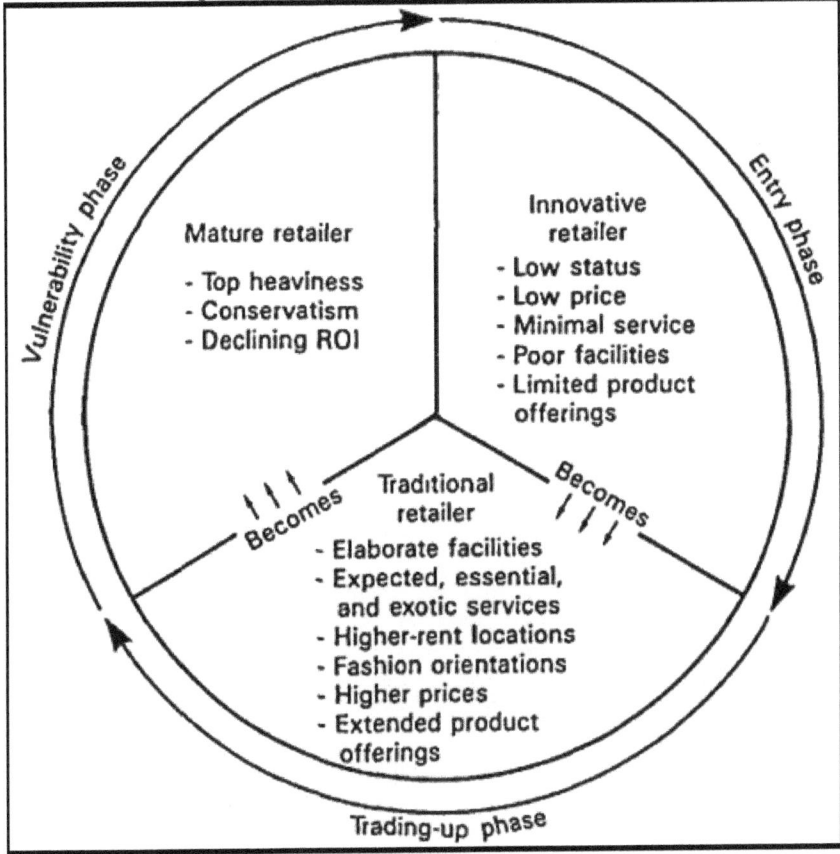

nation. Eventually the founders sold the business, but the new management failed to continue innovating. The store declared bankruptcy in 1991 and again in 1996.

Numerous other retailers have ridden their initial concept to large sales and expanded operations as a result but failed to adapt sufficiently as markets changed. Sears, Kmart, Circuit City (another Richmond retailer), A&P Grocery chain (closed in 2015), and Toys "R" Us are some of the larger retailers to succumb at least partially to the Retail Wheel. Investors lost money as these stocks declined. Investors must watch for changes in the environment that could affect the business of the companies they own.

The Five Stages Every Business Goes Through

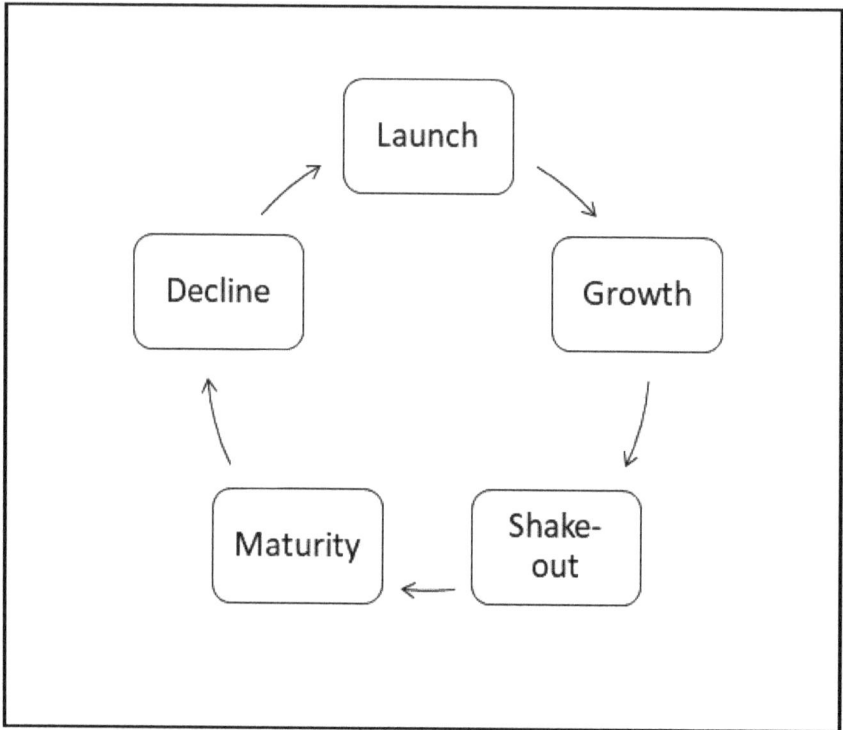

The reason we show this diagram is so you have it handy as you read and think about companies you might want to buy. Some companies will remain viable in their maturity phase because their product is still in demand, and they have continued to keep their products or services viable. Think of automobile manufacturers such as Ford or General Motors. Many packaged products companies have a long history such as Kellogg, Campbell Soup, and General Mills. Our first rule of investing that appears in Chapter Five is to avoid the stocks of companies over 100 years old. Some are still excellent investments, but if you are a new investor, it is best to stick with companies in their growth phase for your early purchases.

Companies that you read about and research are in one of these phases. Firm rules are impossible to map out clearly. Some companies that at first appear to be in their maturity and headed for decline can, with new leadership, reverse course and return to growth. Look at Walmart and Home

Depot over the last fifteen years. They have been fabulous investments for their stockholders.

The key is to be vigilant when selecting stocks. Companies can remake themselves. Later in this book we mention New Era Energy, which is the parent of Florida Power and Light, founded in 1925, but has added many new businesses while maintaining the operations and profits of the foundation firm. It, too, has been and will likely continue to be, a worthwhile holding in portfolios.

If you buy a company when you are young, it may enter the "maturity" phase just as you will. Those are the companies to get out of before they decline too much. Many wonderful companies went too quickly from maturity to decline, and either were purchased by other companies or went bankrupt. Companies in their mature phase often get bought out, usually at a premium, by their competitors. The best example is International Paper which is an amalgamation of numerous paper and lumber companies from Great Northern Nekoosa to Union Camp. Louisiana-Pacific is one of the rare forest-based companies that has remained independent and has raised its stock price somewhat over the years. Forest products are critical for both home builders and paper manufacturers. But owning land that grows trees has not been a path to riches. Trees grow slowly, as some of your stocks may do as well. Airlines have suffered more bankruptcies than any other industry we can think of. These were pioneering firms that, due to many factors—some in their control and some not—went out of business, losing money for shareholders, such as Pan American, Braniff, and Eastern Airlines. Current airlines may have learned their lessons. Airlines remain a cyclical industry.

One caveat to bear in mind is when a company builds a grand edifice during its maturity phase such a splurge *can be* the marker for its next phase of decline. When it went out of business, Pan Am was headquartered in an iconic building in Manhattan that is often seen in the background of old movies. After AT&T built its headquarters, also in Manhattan, the stock has gone nowhere. Here in Central Virginia, Circuit City was not long in its new headquarters before it went out of business. The completion of the Sears Tower in Chicago could have been a signal to let go of that stock. Fortunately, this is not a universal truth, as many companies flourish in their new offices which are needed as the company expands.

Technology has its share of failures but most of those companies can merge with a competitor and survive. The most memorable example was Sun Microsystems founded in 1982. Its stock was a tremendous winner for many investors. It developed and gave away the JAVA programming language which is the basic tool for much current software development. It declined during the "dot-com bubble" of 2000 as its customers stopped ordering its high-end servers. In 2010, Sun was purchased by Oracle Corporation. The point is that, as an investor, you have the *potential* to make most of your money on a stock during its first two phases and, oftentimes, beyond. Just have some idea where your investment lies in the above diagram.

Chapter 4

The Psychology of Investing

Setting up Your Brain

Whether we're talking about socks or stocks, I like buying quality merchandise when it is marked down.

Only buy something that you'd be perfectly happy to hold if the market shut down for 10 years.

You only have to do a very few things right in your life so long as you don't do too many things wrong.

—Warren Buffett quotes

Success in the market involves a specific set of psychological characteristics, including a willingness to take risks; an active imagination; the ability to exercise foresight; and the learned practice of patience. The clichés, unfortunately, obscure these characteristics and make it much more important to fully understand them and intentionally cultivate them.

For starters, as humans we have a set of so-called "normal" behaviors that serve us well in day-to-day life and are firmly imprinted in our minds. We are social creatures who rely on relationships. We are curious and spend time pursuing knowledge and information. We are encultured to work and usually (unless we are wealthy or pursuing a particular dream) have a routine that involves some type of labor. Yet, the psychology of the investor sometimes requires a different kind of thinking that goes against each of these normal tendencies.

A Stern Warning:

Do not buy stock on margin (money/stocks borrowed from your broker). When the market declines, it magnifies your losses because you are still liable for the money (and interest) that sits in your account.

This is not to say that working hard to earn money or conducting research about your investments are not important. There are times, however, when the investor must ignore what is happening with an investment or in the market and intentionally suppress curiosity and worry.

Savvy investors must intentionally retrain their brains in certain important ways. That process often requires going against what is natural, social, intuitive, or normal. It can create cognitive confusion and frustration. One might say, "I work hard at my job, and I get rewarded. Why shouldn't I work hard at investing? People who don't work are lazy, right?"

Yet the investment mindset requires going to strange new places, and sometimes, *not* working hard (intentionally leaving things alone). The good news is that this mindset can be learned through practice the same way people with ADHD can retrain their brains—through cognitive therapies—to be more organized and focused. An example is when portfolio managers tell their clients not to check on their 401ks when the market is in a temporary dip. "Don't even look." All dips historically are temporary, so there is nothing that can be accomplished by bemoaning how much value your account has lost in the last twenty-four hours. It can lead to rash decisions and mistakes. Unless you were unfortunate enough to plan your retirement to begin on the day of the fall, there is nothing to gain by lamenting the temporary loss. In fact, it can interfere with developing your new-investor mindset.

To worry is to be human, yet the psychology of the successful investor must overcome that worry and shape the investor brain to move beyond it. In fact, a properly trained investor will be prepared for the possible scenario above by mitigating it *before* it happens. Market rises and falls are part of the landscape that the successful investor negotiates by expecting these occurrences.

Your hard-earned money matters to you, and why shouldn't you sometimes worry about it? Worrying about money is normal—but constant concern about your investment strategies is a distractor.

This is certainly not a call for developing false confidence. Unexpected events can impact portfolios in dramatic ways. Images of traders jumping out of windows in 1929 come to mind. However, to be ultimately successful as an investor you must plan for the unexpected and accept that some things are beyond your control.

We understand that developing such a mindset is easier said than done. Powerful cultural currents push us away from important elements of it. To cite an example, technology and the development of networks have sped up economic and cultural activity so that the idea of "instant gratification" has become powerfully encultured in our thinking. "Just Google it," is a common expression. The psychology of the successful investor leaves little room for impulsivity, and "just Googling it" has led to more problems than solutions for rash investors.

> *Loss Adversion* is a cognitive bias that explains why individuals feel the pain of loss twice as intensively as the equivalent pleasure of gain. As a result, individuals tend to try to avoid losses in whatever way possible.

American culture also promotes materialism that leads to the pursuit of more trappings of wealth— bigger car, bigger house, faster laptop, more expensive smartphone—and while all of these things serve their purposes and are goods of "value" in the strictest sense, this materialistic mindset must be banished from the psychology of the investor. Yes, being successful as an investor can allow you to buy a bigger house, but the goal is to succeed as an investor, not as an owner of a bigger house. The subtlety might seem unimportant but is vital to understanding the investor mindset.

Once you as an investor begin to understand the social forces at work and adjust your mindset to minimize their effects, you will likely be surprised at how you're thinking about investment begins to clarify. Some people are more gifted naturally with this ability but, like any skill, it can be learned. We are not talking about you becoming a different person. Rather, we will show you a different way to think about one aspect of your life.

Another element of this psychology is the legendary "sixth sense" that some famous investors seemed to possess. Surely, some might say that ability can't be taught or learned. In fact, part of developing investor psychology is the conscious decision to seek gestalt—like the instincts of Antiques Roadshow appraisers mentioned above. An example of gestalt psychology in everyday life is in the way people complete jigsaw puzzles. Rather than looking at each piece as an individual unit, they form meaningful relationships between the pieces to see the big picture more quickly and efficiently. The economy is the finished puzzle. Each stock is a piece in that wide puzzle. Successful investing requires the ability to study the market in detail, while positioning such detail in the sweeping trends at the national and global levels. This skill is what some call the sixth sense, but it can be learned.

Another cultural force working against the successful investor is the trend that delimits the importance of reading. In the near past, investors had to read to accumulate the level of detail necessary to achieve gestalt. Now, detail is pushed into our daily lives in unending abundance through social media and technology. Newspapers and journals increasingly exist only in the virtual world. Unfortunately, the successful investor in the twenty-first century must fight against this virtual information glut and continue to read. Achieving gestalt is not possible without acquiring specific information about a company or person, and reading is still the most effective way to sort through the details.

One reason one might pay someone to manage their portfolio is that they *don't* have to read. Thus, it may seem that the successful investor who manages his own portfolio is a weird person—we don't want a bigger house; we still read: we don't allow ourselves to be distracted by social media; we are not seeking instant gratification; and we map out time to do nothing but think. A successful investor is weird, and that is why there aren't many of them comparatively speaking. In our culture we are wealthy enough that most people have someone, or an entity, who looks after their retirement and pensions with relative success, but the individual who would become a successful investor faces an uphill battle. Developing the right psychology is key.

Another characteristic of successful investors is resiliency. In fact, some psychologists believe this may be the single most important personality trait for success in many areas of life, such as education and relationships. Resiliency is the ability to bounce back from bumps in the road. This will be a critical part of a later chapter on what to do when things go wrong (which they always do at some point).

Related to this is the importance of positivity or optimism. We are trained in our culture to associate the minus sign with something bad (-), and the plus sign with things that are good (+). The same goes for red (bad) and green (good). Anyone with an E*TRADE or similar account already knows that you feel bad when you see losses or feel good when you see gains. This mindset is human nature, but the psychology of the investor requires a different way of thinking.

You Don't Know What It Was Like

One of the authors is old enough to remember the recessions of the 1970s and 80s. Paul Volker was appointed Federal Reserve Chairman by President Jimmy Carter in 1979 and was reappointed by Ronald Reagan. The Federal Reserve raised interest rates in a Draconian manner to force inflation out of the economy. The Volker Bear market of 1980 resulted in the Dow Jones Industrial Average closing at 776.92 on August 12, 1982. Today it is over 40,000. The market moved straight up in the fall of 1982. But when you look at the Dow from 1982 until today, it's been a wild ride.

On any given day you are investing in a sliver of time. The only thing we can say is that the market rises and falls. Down feels terrible and makes you want to run away. We think it feels like a movie when the hero, while visiting a foreign country, is taken to jail for no obvious reason. There, he is alone in a cold cell with no visitors until the authorities drag him out and take him for interrogation. In investing, this process can go on for a long time. But at least one of your stocks at some time will be "arrested" by the market and tortured. It will go down and down and down without any explanation or hope of getting out. Then one day someone comes and says you are free to go. No explanation or apology is given. Keep this in mind when you receive a short-term sentence or one that can last over a year. You did nothing wrong, yet you are the one in pain. Selling would end the pain, but sometimes it is better to endure the pain and wait for the market to stop its persecution of your investment. There are times when sitting with a declining stock creates a dilemma. As before, imagine you owned Boeing stock in October 2020 when it began its decline. You don't know how far it will fall. One way to deal with this situation would be to sell off a few shares to relieve the pressure. While there is no general rule, you could sell some of the stock and switch that money into a stock with a long-term upward trend such as Welltower. Boeing will take years to return to its former level of operational excellence. Taking a loss and switching to a stock with better prospects is sometimes the best solution.

> Buying a stock while it is in decline is called *catching a falling knife.*

Any portfolio will do better over time. Many studies prove this again and again. Missing just a few of the best days of gains during a year severely impacts a portfolio's gains. You cannot predict market moves. Therefore, getting in and out quickly has not been proven to produce better results.

> *Investing in stocks appears to be a very attractive option for long-term investors. The historical equity premium in the United States is quite large (Mehra and Prescott, 1985). Conventional wisdom is that stocks are safe over long holding periods, and long-term loss realizations in the US have been infrequent or non-existent (see, e.g., Siegel, 2014). Fama and French (2018a) estimate a low probability of loss and a high probability of substantial gain for investors with horizons of 20 or 30 years.*
>
> From *Journal of Financial Economics*
> **Volume 143, Issue 1, January 2022**

Sometimes, when listening to podcasts, interviews on *Finance.Yahoo.com* or watching CNBC you feel as if you have walked into a party where others have already spent hours enjoying themselves and getting to know each other. You feel as if you're the only sober person in the room, the designated driver. The market is a fast-paced environment. Information is flying around every second. Those who make decisions and those who run mutual funds find they need to utilize quantitative tools and let computers make the decisions. At the company level, humans still make the decisions. Business relies on computers, science, and analysis more than ever, but there are still humans in these chains. Don't despair. Step back or step up when you're ready. In other words, we often must go against our instincts as this chapter emphasizes, thinking beyond red and green, pluses and minuses, good and bad, etc. It is difficult, but the investor brain can be retrained.

Peter Lynch, the legendary manager of the Fidelity Magellan Fund between 1977 and 1990, wrote *One Up on Wall Street* in 1989. It can serve also as a background for investing. Many of the companies he discusses no longer exist, have gone bankrupt, or merged with other companies so imagine, equally, inserting the companies we discuss into his same narrative. The rules he describes still hold, such as his observation, "When you invest in stocks, you must have a basic faith in human nature, in capitalism, in the country at large, and in future prosperity in general. So far, nothing's been strong enough to shake me out of it." He also admits to always being fully invested. The Magellan Fund during his tenure produced an astonishing 29.2 percent annual return, but he sadly points out that many investors bought and redeemed shares too quickly. This is because of the factors outlined above. One must have determination to survive both good times and bad. During recessions a chemical company, for example, can't turn itself into a chocolate factory that might not face the same fall-off in demand as the need for polyethylene falls during downturns. Sometimes, an investor must maintain a foxhole mentality until conditions improve. As Baron de Rothschild, who made a fortune buying in the panic that followed the Battle of Waterloo against Napoleon, is reported to have said, "Buy when there's blood in the streets, even if the blood is your own." More recently, Warren Buffett warns, "You pay a very high price in the stock market for a cheery consensus." In other words, if everyone says the stock market will continue to rise for the next six months, be wary, or if everyone says buy Apple as is currently the case on the eve of its 4-for-1 stock split, look out. Apple stock will be higher by the time anyone reads this book, but it won't double again as it has over the last ten months (October 2019 - August 2020.) Temper your enthusiasm, but do not expect the market will go to zero either. We live most of our lives between extreme happiness and what we think is unendurable sadness. At the bottom, at your darkest hour, you will discover things always get better—or the stock market is not for you.

Benefits from this Chapter

From Raj Bhatia, Merrill Lynch Private Wealth Management

Panic selling is a sign of poor planning because markets have moved significantly many times in the past forty years. It's nothing new if you look at the history of markets...in this business [managing your own portfolio, survivng is winning. And being able to navigate all the ups and downs of the market, all the faces of cleints [your family and yourself] and all these regulations is challenging.

Part II

Stocks to Buy
Assessing a Stock
and Buying It

Chapter 5

Your First Day in the Stock Market

Confusion, Fear, then Clarity

I believe it's strikingly important to remember that when you know better, you can do better. With higher levels of awareness, you can make smarter choices. And the more clarity you get as to who you want to become, the quicker you can start making the choices needed to get you there.

—Robin S. Sharma

Imagine this is your first trip to Tokyo. You are on a subway platform and get separated from your group. You don't have a map or directions for where to go. Of course, you do not speak the language. It's the same if you have never invested in the stock market. You don't know how to buy stocks or which one to buy. The logical choice is to give someone your money and say, "Take me somewhere." But we suggest you learn the language, read about the area, talk to people, listen, and discover. Then you'll know which stocks to buy or which train to take to your destination.

> Small investors are minnows swimming with whales. The journey can be perilous for an individual since others often have access to more resources. But an individual can learn from history and from selecting, buying and selling stocks. An old adage says:
>
> *The stongest storms make the best sailors.*
> Sail on!

Stock Language

Stocks have a language of their own. One day they will speak to you! Stocks are more than symbols on the computer screen. They have a history. Companies have people working every day to improve the business. They may even have a founder still working at the company (those are the best companies). People wake up every day, prepare their lunch, apply their skills all day, and then go home to their families. This is what makes America's industry (and industries in other countries) great: people working hard to succeed for themselves, their families, and their company. You want to find the best of these and buy their stocks.

There are thousands of stocks for sale at any given moment, and you must choose the best one(s) for you. On July 6, 2020, Merrill Lynch updated their price target for Fox Factory Holding Corporation (FOXF) to $93 a share from $90. It was a stock on our watchlist. It may be one to follow. That's what you will do. Hear or read about a stock and then watch it and accumulate money to buy it when that stock reaches a point where you think you should own it. There is no rush with a stock like this. Five years ago on July 6, 2015, it was $15.79 a share. Unfortunately, we didn't own it. In July of 2017 it was about $37 a share. That's the way stocks grow. They grow like something you plant in your yard. But checking again in July 2024 the stock was around $50 a share. It peaked at $183 in 2021. Shareholders have not made money on this stock in a long time. We would have given up after that peak. But when would it be safe to get back in? It's a good company in an industry where it's hard to increase prices, we would guess. This would have to be researched to see if it made sense now to buy it. Companies face constant storms during their existence.

On the following pages is a picture of how Fox Factory Holdings did between 2015 and 2020.

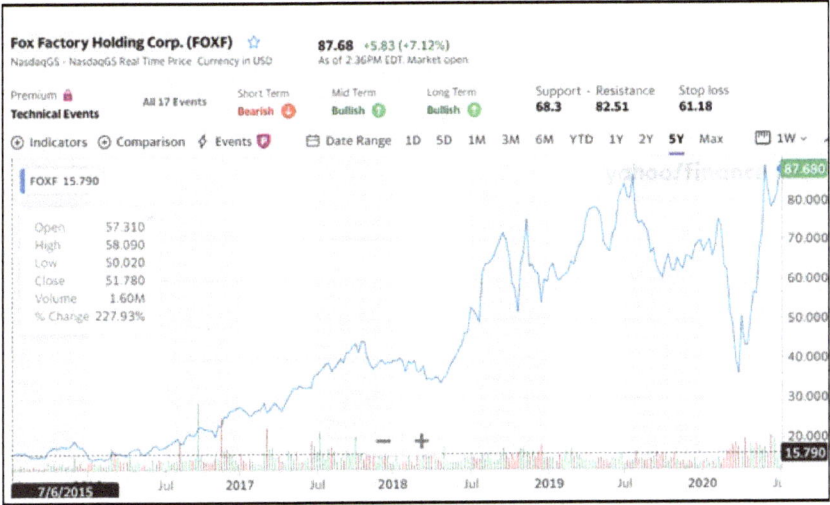

Fox Factory Holding Corp. (FOXF) ☆
NasdaqGS · NasdaqGS Real Time Price. Currency in USD
87.68 +5.83 (+7.12%)
As of 2:36PM EDT. Market open

Premium 🔒		Short Term	Mid Term	Long Term	Support - Resistance		Stop loss
Technical Events	All 17 Events	Bearish 🔻	Bullish 🔼	Bullish 🔼	68.3	82.51	61.18

⊙ Indicators ⊙ Comparison ✐ Events 🚩   ▦ Date Range 1D 5D 1M 3M 6M YTD 1Y 2Y **5Y** Max   1W ⌄

FOXF 15.790	
Open	57.310
High	58.090
Low	50.020
Close	51.780
Volume	1.60M
% Change	227.93%

The company has had challenges and weak earnings during the last five years. Hence the stock went down.

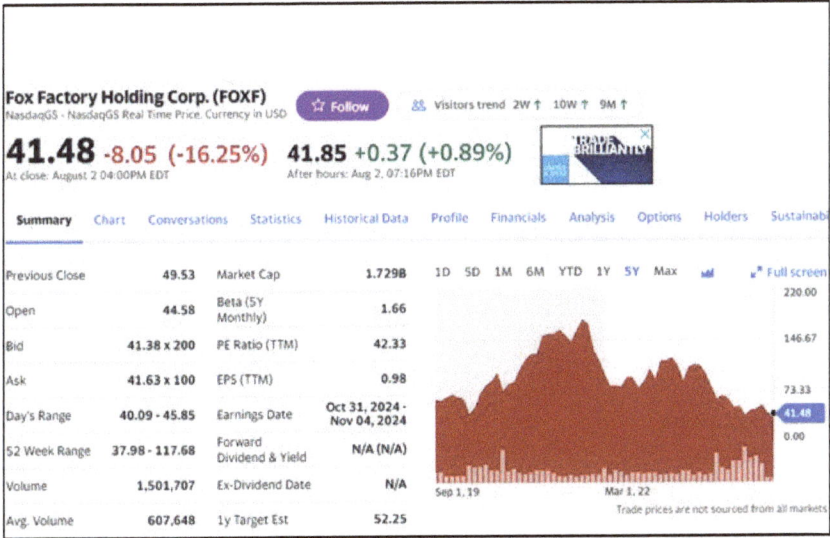

Fox Factory Holding Corp. (FOXF) ☆ Follow   👁 Visitors trend 2W ↑ 10W ↑ 9M ↑
NasdaqGS - NasdaqGS Real Time Price. Currency in USD

41.48 -8.05 (-16.25%)   41.85 +0.37 (+0.89%)
At close: August 2 04:00PM EDT   After hours: Aug 2, 07:16PM EDT

Summary Chart Conversations Statistics Historical Data Profile Financials Analysis Options Holders Sustainab

Previous Close	49.53	Market Cap	1.729B
Open	44.58	Beta (5Y Monthly)	1.66
Bid	41.38 x 200	PE Ratio (TTM)	42.33
Ask	41.63 x 100	EPS (TTM)	0.98
Day's Range	40.09 - 45.85	Earnings Date	Oct 31, 2024 - Nov 04, 2024
52 Week Range	37.98 - 117.68	Forward Dividend & Yield	N/A (N/A)
Volume	1,501,707	Ex-Dividend Date	N/A
Avg. Volume	607,648	1y Target Est	52.25

In 2020, we were fortunate we had not bought this stock when it was on a tear but now might be a good time to buy it. We would still need to watch it to see if earnings will come back.

Now, let's look at another similar stock in our friend's portfolio—Equinix (EQIX).

July 6, 2020
Initial purchase August 20, 2012
(*fractional shares were due to dividends paid in stock instead of cash)

› EQIX ⓘ	Trade ⌄ 🔔 ☰₊	722.11	3.70	0.52%	26.79586	194.3867	99.14	14,140.80

The chart below shows it took almost nine years for this stock to get this high. But it rose almost continuously while she owned it.

The point of these examples is to imagine, as Warren Buffet does, that you are buying the whole company. Another option, once you decide a company is good enough for you to invest in, is to buy additional shares when it is down. Dollar-cost averaging over time is a great way to accumulate wealth. Jim Cramer's advice from his books is to purchase the total amount of stock you planned to buy but in chunks over time.

Equinix Stock Chart 2012 – 2020 when we sold it

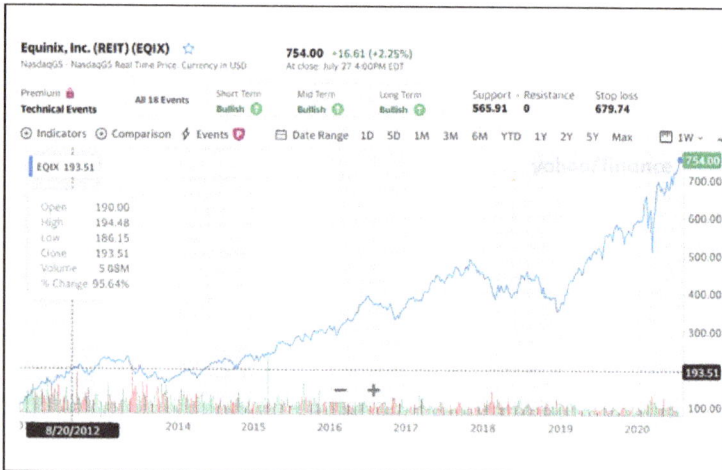

Be warned that on the first day you finally buy a stock, most likely it will go down. An initial purchase is a flip of a coin. It's just the way the market works. If you buy a stock and it goes up, count yourself lucky. But ultimately it has nothing to do with you. The market treats us all the same. We show up at the window, place our bets, and the horse will win or lose on any given day. But by selecting companies with good prospects, the winnings will occur over future days.

We have presented two stocks that caught our eye on July 6, 2020. Equinix is in a portfolio that we advise a friend on. We recommended the purchase of Equinix in 2012. The other one was brought to our attention in Merrill Lynch's daily list of analyst updates. Both are good companies; one was a good stock, the other failed to rise (Fox Factory Holdings). But where will they be in five years?

The question is what else is there to buy besides these two? If our friend didn't already own Equinix, we would not recommend she purchase it. It already has a market cap of $64 billion. It will not likely double again in the next nine years. It will probably continue to raise its dividend, however. For her, it became a harvest candidate for the next time she needs some cash. Additionally, in the same space several similar businesses may have better growth prospects such as Digital Realty Trust (DLR) and CyrusOne (CONE). The reason for this is that small portfolios that individuals own should only hold one of each kind of business or industry. Be sure you're not doubling up in the same industry unless you have a very good reason to do so.

Sidebar: Digital Realty Trust has risen less than fifty percent in the last five years. CyrusOne was acquired by Kolberg Kravis Roberts (KKR) in 2022. Equinix in mid-2024 was around $800 a share. We sold it at the right time because our friend needed money. Luckily, it was dead money for several years after that. We did not foresee the future. It just seemed time to sell it.

Don't chase a stock by buying it at a high and higher price. Be patient until it drops lower from where it is today. It may not drop as low as you hope, but it will come down enough to offer you a better entry point that improves your chances of making a profit. Exercise *nài xīn*, the patience of a Mandarin. Wait for it. If the drop never comes, move on to another opportunity.

Fox Factory Holdings only has a $3.5 billion market cap. Not everyone will buy a mountain bike, but the population will continue to rise, and other demographics support the company's continued expansion. It becomes one to watch as a candidate for purchase since it will likely continue to grow. It's simply easier to grow a smaller company than a larger one.

Neither Equinix nor Fox Factory Holdings will be bantered about on the business news. Today, Apple, Microsoft, Google, and Nvidia all get the press. Everyone already knows about them.

That doesn't mean you shouldn't buy them, only that many others are already looking at them. They are too expensive for most of us plus their growth projections can't go on forever. The average investor should be wary of stocks that keep climbing and climbing without careful examination. At the rate companies like Apple and Amazon are projected to grow, they could wipe out all their competitors. Just use your instincts and common sense.

There is an eye-opening video by Warren Buffett on YouTube called "Warren Buffett on the Evolution of the World's Largest Companies." He begins his presentation with a list of the twenty largest companies in 1989, remarking that not one of them is on the list in 2021. What is on top today may not be on top thirty years from now.

If all this sounds confusing, it is. Thousands of stocks are each blown by a different wind. Each company faces its own influences and circumstances. We cannot judge a company with a single yardstick, and we cannot foresee every outcome. We can only conduct research and make an assessment with the knowledge acquired. If you select a stock that goes down, you must make another assessment to either sell and let it go or make a bold decision to hold on to it and give it time to grow. If a stock doesn't show signs of going up or correcting course, then sell it, but give it time first.

Use This Key Metric To Start Your Search

Merrill Lynch offers competitor information on their recommendations, such as Morningstar and CFRA (Center for Financial Research and Analysis) both well-regarded research operations. Morningstar is a bit more conservative so when it shows a five-star rating on a stock, pay attention. CFRA was formerly the research arm of Standard and Poor. It too uses a five-star rating system while Merrill Lynch only uses Buy-Hold-Sell rankings. CFRA has a piece of information that can be extremely useful in their reports. They show how much $10,000 invested five years ago in the stock of the company they are reviewing would be worth today. Here is an example from a report on NextEra Energy:

Stock Report | **August 22, 2020** | NYSE Symbol: **NEE** | **NEE** is in the S&P 500

NextEra Energy, Inc.

CFRA

Recommendation **HOLD** ★★★☆☆	Price USD 282.41 *(as of market close Aug 21, 2020)*	12-Mo. Target Price USD 297.00	Report Currency USD	Investment Style Large-Cap Blend
Equity Analyst				

GICS Sector Utilities	**Summary** NextEra Energy, Inc. (formerly FPL Group) is the holding company for Florida Power & Light,
Sub-Industry Electric Utilities	Gulf Power and NextEra Energy Resources.

Key Stock Statistics [Source: CFRA, S&P Global Market Intelligence (SPGMI), Company Reports]

52-Wk Range	USD 287.78 - 181.66	Oper.EPS2020E	USD 9.13	Market Capitalization(B)	USD 138.28	Beta	0.22
Trailing 12-Month EPS	USD 7.24	Oper.EPS2021E	USD 9.87	Yield [%]	1.98	3-yr Proj. EPS CAGR[%]	7
Trailing 12-Month P/E	39.01	P/E on Oper EPS2020E	30.93	Dividend Rate/Share	USD 5.6	SPGMI's Quality Ranking	A
$10K Invested 5 Yrs Ago	$30,740.0	Common Shares Outstg.[M]	480.00	Institutional Ownership [%]	79.0		

We recommend looking for companies that can grow roughly 15% a year. At that rate, the stock doubles in five years. For NextEra Energy to have yielded $30,740 it had to grow 32.5% a year on average. That is an extraordinary return. Domino's Pizza stock grew $10,000 to $36,024 in just five years. Apple grew $10,000 to $42,639 in the last five-year period. Few stocks achieve these kinds of metrics. A stalwart company like Bristol-Myers Squibb hardly grew at all with only $11,076 over five years while Citigroup's stock declined and turned $10,000 into $9,971. But this is looking backward. Never forget the disclaimer that "past performance is no guarantee of future results." The analysts at Merrill Lynch and CFRA expect that Citigroup will return to a growth trajectory once the economy improves.

We would not expect Apple, Domino's Pizza, or NextEra Energy to duplicate those numbers over the next five years. Their returns were higher than most companies' but be aware that looking back is only part of your research. We can think of many companies that did not repeat extraordinary past performance. The long-term view often works out unless the industry collapses as has happened to companies that produce petroleum products. The challenging thing to determine is what the next five years will produce. Overall, companies that grew well in the last five years will grow at an above-average rate because they operate on an established business model. Anything can go wrong, but they will probably excel.

After looking at the past returns of the above stocks, we found that in August 2020, CFRA gave them four-star ratings. In other words, CFRA believes that Dominos, Apple, Citigroup, Disney, and Bristol-Myers Squibb will gain at an equal pace over the next year. Who can see farther than that? If a stock has lagged recently, it may indeed perform better in the future. By 2024, Citigroup, Disney, and Bristol-Myers Squibb lagged the market. The good news is that even if a stock did not grow at rates predicted by analysts, they usually stay flat.

The point is that you are stepping into a kind of mess on any given day in the stock market, but don't turn and run away. Instead think of it as an opportunity. Start with how a stock has done over its last five years. Next, research its prospects for the next five years. Then buy or move on to another stock. There are markers to indicate which stocks are likely to do well over the next five years. We will cover this in the following chapters.

So, we advise you to pick the best stocks you can with the highest growth rate you could expect and buy those companies. But also, diversify because they will not all achieve the rates you expect.

The Rule of Seventy-Two

Another useful tool is the Rule of Seventy-Two: how long it will take a stock to double given an expected rate of return. Imagine what you expect will be the rate of return on the stock(s) you research. Suppose you bought Dominion Energy, the utility serving the region where we live. If you think the return with the dividend and earnings growth would be 8%, then divide 72 by 8. The result is 9. It will take 9 years for the stock including dividends to double. Suppose you think Fox Factory Holdings can grow at 12% a year? Divide 72 by 12 and you will discover that FOXF will double in six years. For stock to double in five years, it needs to achieve a 15% growth rate, which is very hard to achieve.

Investment Guideline 1

Imagine you are buying stock for a daughter, son or grandchild so they can buy their first home. Buy reasonably priced, normally growing stocks. Expect your stocks to hit singles and doubles. Do not expect a homerun.
Then be patient. Don't give up and sell it too quickly.

After You Buy a Stock, What Happens?

The chances of a stock you purchase falling in value the day after you purchase it is 50-50. On any given day, buying stock is like flipping a coin. The price can go up or go down. Only over time will the fundamental drivers of a company's stock price determine the real value of the stock. During the time, say two years, that you first own a stock, the price pattern will resemble a sawtooth mountain range provided the stock has additional earnings. It rises a little and may fall a lot. But if the product or service is sound and solid, the price will rise and rise. During the months you own it, many factors such as economic or competitive pressures, or changes in institutions' buying patterns will make a stock go down from time to time. It is discomforting and requires you to maintain ultimate faith in the stock you purchased. Give it time to show you what it can do. You may have a racehorse, and in the third year you own it you will discover what it can do.

We have friends who simply tire of their stock languishing and say, "it's not going to do anything," and sell it before it has had a chance to report earnings for several quarters. During the time you own a stock, you will want to keep an eye on financial news and analysts' reports after the company reports earnings. You would not enroll your child in a French class and expect her to be fluent in the language after six months. The managers and employees of the company wake every day, go to work, and apply themselves diligently to their tasks. The main point is that you must give the companies time to show you they were worth your investment. New employees get a paycheck after about a month on the job. Stockholders must wait longer. Build a mental runway long enough to allow the company to show you what it can do.

Do not get over-euphoric over a stock you own that has gone up a lot recently. Likewise, do not become despondent about a stock you own that has languished in value. Companies rise and fall. You cannot avoid all losses or catch all the gains. Keep a clear head and ask some fundamental questions before buying more or dumping it all. Small gains in the middle tier of companies may be better for your portflio than swinging for the fences.

What about Artificial Intelligence in Mid-2024?

We opened the preface with the statement that you must make an investment in AI semiconductors and the companies that make them. But when? They are already up by an astounding amount. Will they continue to rise? Will an investor be able to make money on stocks like Nvidia, Apple, Microsoft, Micron, or any of the related stocks from this point on?

The answer is yes, but you can only purchase small amounts when these stocks decline or when you are brave enough to make additional purchases as they rise. Why do we suggest this strategy? Because this may be a once-in-a-lifetime opportunity, and these companies are doing impressive things. It makes sense to own some of them. You are like a general trying to decide whether to commit your troops to battle or wait for a better opportunity. Owning stocks sometimes requires bravery and guts. Just do your best. We will discuss this again in the concluding chapter.

Your Best Advantage Starting Out

When your portfolio is small, you can better handle losses because losses are minimal. If you have a good stock that falls in price, you can either buy more or sell it. But if you are in your first year of investing, it will not derail your progress. Diversify, stay the course, and either repair the damage or take the loss in stride. Do not lose sleep over it.

Chapter 6

What are the Best Recipes
for Stocks to Buy?

(What You've Been Waiting For)

No one who cooks, cooks alone. Even at her most solitary, a cook in the kitchen is surrounded by generations of cooks past, the advice and menus of cooks present, the wisdom of cookbook writers. **—Laurie Colwin**

I cook with wine; sometimes I even add it to the food. **— W.C. Fields**

...no one is born a great cook, one learns by doing. **— Julia Child**

When you're on the run all the time, you may feel like there is no time to cook/invest. Of course you can eat out/use a broker. But there are ways you can also cook a quick, easy meal for yourself. Here's a simple recipe:

- Go to Merrill Lynch (*ML.com*—you must have an account there) and click on analysts' recommendations or E*TRADE, or whatever brokerage you decide to use.

- Look at the most recent posts (There are a *lot* otherwise).

- Read the taglines for the most recent comments.

- Decide if one of them looks promising based on CFRA or

Morningstar aligning with Merrill Lynch's opinion (many public libraries subscribe to these).

- Buy a *few* shares.
- Follow weekly updates but do not act immediately (refrigerate).

This is a recipe for when you are on the fly, but it usually keeps well in the fridge/buy at a later date. You may want to buy more down the line. You cannot give every investment all the time and research you might want to. There are thousands of publicly traded stocks. It is the same phenomenon you experience when you go down the aisles of your local supermarket. If you want to make chili, you arrive first at the shelves with diced tomatoes. Each label lists various cuts, extra spices, and other variations. Imagine they are companies offering communication software. How do you pick? We check out the various stocks with one of the advisory services that we subscribe to such as E*TRADE, Merrill Lynch, Morningstar, or Motley Fool. Not every stock is covered by every service provider, but you can find something. Let's look at a popular stock, United Health Care.

E*TRADE lists numerous analysts who cover United Health Care. What this shows is that they all agree the company will do well. In 2020, they provided a more detailed report from their preferred partner, Credit Suisse.

Now at the end of July—July 30, 2024—we have a chart from Yahoo Finance. It shows a long rise in stock price year after year. It shows that United Healthcare has almost doubled in the last five years. There were some periods when it declined. Do not abandon good companies when they decline if nothing fundamental has changed.

Getting Started

It's time to prepare to buy some stocks. Here is our plan for your first year. Depending on how much money you can invest, set up your account and accumulate or deposit at least $500. Once you have that minimal amount, you can purchase some stock. The vision we have is that you will start small and add to your investments until you reach a sizeable portfolio over several decades. At that point, you would reassess your goals. You can keep managing your own money and adding mutual funds, give it to an adviser to handle the headaches, or simply sit back and do other things and let the stocks grow. Entrepreneurs do not go into business to reach just their short-term or intermediate goals. They begin the business to succeed and succeed again. Here in Virginia, Richard Fairbank founded Capital One in 1988 with the support of Richmond, Virginia-based Signet Bank. Thirty-six years later, he is still the CEO of the company that has evolved into a bank as well as a credit card company. Even with the pandemic of 2020 the company in 2024 is still worth $76 billion. Think like an owner.

Your first stock, hopefully one you will hold for five years or more, should be a company that provides a product or service that people use every single day. Consider companies such as Kroger, Comcast, Bank of America, PayPal, Domino's Pizza, or Netflix. What *not* to do applies as well. If a stock has had a story break in the news and all over the financial pages, then avoid that stock. Similarly, one rule we have uncovered is *not* to buy stocks of companies that have been in business for over 100 years (see previous chapter). This is a general rule to help you avoid companies that are carrying baggage from an earlier century that can drag down their future performance. But this may not apply to a company such as NextEra Energy which, because it owns Florida Power and Light, is approaching 100 years old but is heavily oriented to new energy alternatives. There are so many vibrant, young companies to choose from that you can avoid old companies for most of your purchases. There are companies that have been around for a long time that have reshaped what they do, so they may be good future investments. This advice is meant as a caution, but you will want to perform your own due diligence.

The benefit of buying a large, well-regarded stock as your first purchase is that it can be easier to get updates on it. Also, it will likely pay a dividend and give you some small return. Another benefit is that its price may fluctuate less than the stocks of smaller capitalization companies. It is a way to learn how to swim by getting in the shallow end first before considering other kinds of stocks that are not as well known. Here, with a company like VISA or United Healthcare, you can still hold on to the edge of the pool, see the ladder, and get the feel for the temperature of the water before going deeper.

Jack's Recipe For "One in the Barrel"

In former times, fish were caught, salted, and then stored in barrels. It wasn't the same as eating fresh fish just off the hook, but it was better than being in a place where no fish were available. "One in the barrel" meant that you were saving it for a time when there were no fresh fish.

We have made the case to avoid companies that are too old, or too established by reputation rather than performance, or have services and products going out of date. Here's a recipe:

Research stocks that are at least five years old, but less than ten years old. This becomes your "fish in the barrel": relatively new but tested and preserved.

Scan this list and choose one that fits the criteria you are developing for the dozen or so stocks in your portfolio.

Buy a modest number of shares (no more than 10% of your overall account).

Watch and wait but remember not to wait forever; even fish in the barrel will eventually go bad!

If you are not 100% sure about a stock, then just wait. The stock market is open every business day. It's not like a special house that you have seen on your way to work for years and suddenly there is a "For Sale" sign in the yard. Instead, put the stock in the barrel or on a "watchlist" you maintain inside your brokerage account. A fish in the barrel is also a colloquialism for something easy to do!

The Most Important Lesson We Learned

Rather than keeping you in suspense until the last page, here is the revelation we have discovered: buy companies that have a solid business model that sustains them through all sorts of business and competitor challenges. This model is so simple we don't see why we didn't find and follow it a long time ago. Buy companies that show growth and increased earnings year-after-year. You're thinking *duh, that's no revelation*. Let's talk about specifics. The reason we didn't catch on before is that as mere humans we focus too much attention on the short-term prices and news items about a stock. For decades Berkshire Hathaway has grown as Warren Buffet continued to extol the virtues of holding stocks "forever." Investors of our fathers' generation said the same thing—buy and hold. As a young man, one of us once asked a salesperson who called on the company I worked for when to sell a stock. The reply was *I never sell*. He was confident that good companies would weather the challenges and obstacles that came at them.

Apple and Microsoft have been outstanding performers for decades. These companies keep doing things right. Even when Steve Jobs passed away, Apple did not crash and burn. The company has an innovation culture that has guided it since the founder died and prior to that.

Potential Purchases for Your First Stock

Here are companies whose stocks show gains over the five years or more that you may want to investigate. This is a conservative list. We exclude technology since you can easily research those companies on their websites. You don't want a company that can flourish only when it has a CEO culture because it can fail after that singularly excellent CEO leaves or retires. Think of General Electric after Jack Welch left. Look for great companies, not just great CEOs. Here's our list:

- Ameriprise (AMP)
- BJ's Wholesale Club Holdings (BJ) or Costco (COST)
- D. R. Horton (DHI)
- Chemed Corporation (CHE)
- Amphenol Corporation (APH)
- Thermo Fisher Scientific (TMO)
- United Rentals (URI)
- Eli Lilly (LLY), Merck (MRK) or United Health Care (UNH)
- Progressive Insurance (PGH)
- Tractor Supply (TSCO)
- Walmart (WMT)

Research these and others like them. Look at price charts for several years. They can be found on *Finace.Yahoo.com*. There are many others like them. Ask yourself what elements a great company has. Discover what makes it stand out. Additionally, compare these charts to the price of those same stocks today to decide which ones made the best return if you had owned them.

You might also purchase others that meet the same criteria, such as Nvidia, Broadcom, and other tech names that are written about in the news daily and have become household names. Regardless of the stock(s) you pick on this list you will have to ride them through ups and downs, buying when they fall. You are looking for companies with a chart like this chart for Broadcom (AVGO) on the next page.

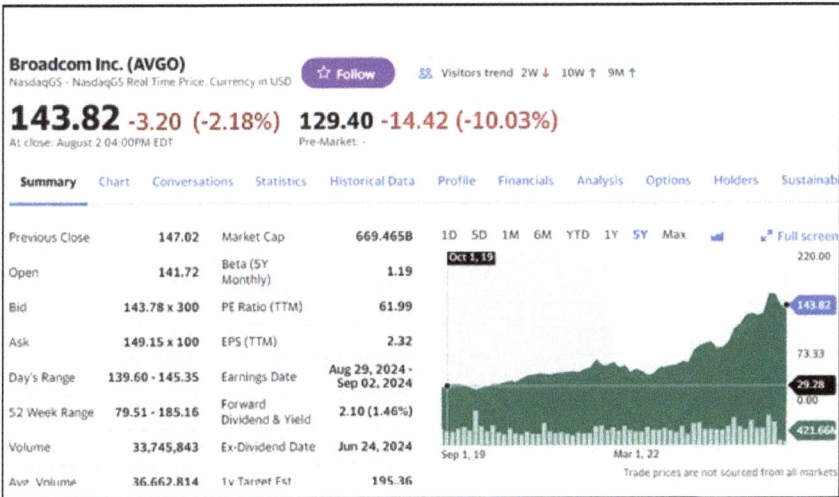

Broadcom Inc. (AVGO)
NasdaqGS - NasdaqGS Real Time Price. Currency in USD

143.82 -3.20 (-2.18%) **129.40** -14.42 (-10.03%)
At close: August 2 04:00PM EDT   Pre-Market: -

| Summary | Chart | Conversations | Statistics | Historical Data | Profile | Financials | Analysis | Options | Holders | Sustainab |

Previous Close	147.02	Market Cap	669.465B
Open	141.72	Beta (5Y Monthly)	1.19
Bid	143.78 x 300	PE Ratio (TTM)	61.99
Ask	149.15 x 100	EPS (TTM)	2.32
Day's Range	139.60 - 145.35	Earnings Date	Aug 29, 2024 - Sep 02, 2024
52 Week Range	79.51 - 185.16	Forward Dividend & Yield	2.10 (1.46%)
Volume	33,745,843	Ex-Dividend Date	Jun 24, 2024
Avg. Volume	36,662,814	1y Target Est	195.36

Steer clear of companies such as APA Corporation (APA), which is in the energy producing sector. While we hold it, it is for their long-term venture in Suriname. See the chart below.

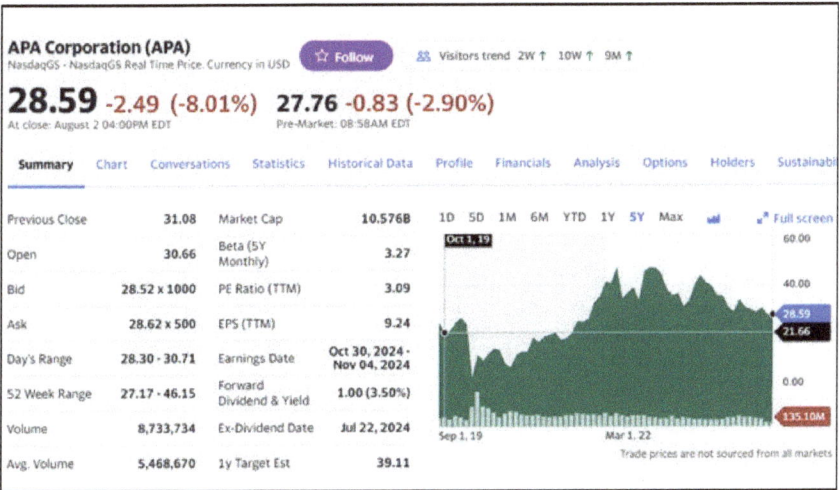

APA Corporation (APA)
NasdaqGS - NasdaqGS Real Time Price. Currency in USD

28.59 -2.49 (-8.01%) **27.76** -0.83 (-2.90%)
At close: August 2 04:00PM EDT   Pre-Market: 08:58AM EDT

| Summary | Chart | Conversations | Statistics | Historical Data | Profile | Financials | Analysis | Options | Holders | Sustainab |

Previous Close	31.08	Market Cap	10.576B
Open	30.66	Beta (5Y Monthly)	3.27
Bid	28.52 x 1000	PE Ratio (TTM)	3.09
Ask	28.62 x 500	EPS (TTM)	9.24
Day's Range	28.30 - 30.71	Earnings Date	Oct 30, 2024 - Nov 04, 2024
52 Week Range	27.17 - 46.15	Forward Dividend & Yield	1.00 (3.50%)
Volume	8,733,734	Ex-Dividend Date	Jul 22, 2024
Avg. Volume	5,468,670	1y Target Est	39.11

We can list a hundred companies. The key is to add to your portfolio well-run companies in businesses that allow them to achieve repeatable earnings over time. Warren Buffet owns both Chevron (CVX) and Occidental Petroleum (OXY) but their charts do not look as good as Thermo Fisher's. It's important to own stocks that allow you to sleep at night.

Buy List of Long-Term Stocks

These were screenshots taken before the market opened on a particularly disastrous day, August 2, 2024.

BJ's Wholesale Club Holdings, Inc. (BJ)
NYSE - Nasdaq Real Time Price. Currency in USD
☆ Follow   👥 Visitors trend 2W ↑ 10W ↑ 9M ↑

86.85 -0.95 (-1.08%)   **84.23** -2.62 (-3.01%)
At close: August 2 04:00PM EDT   Pre-Market: 09:06AM EDT

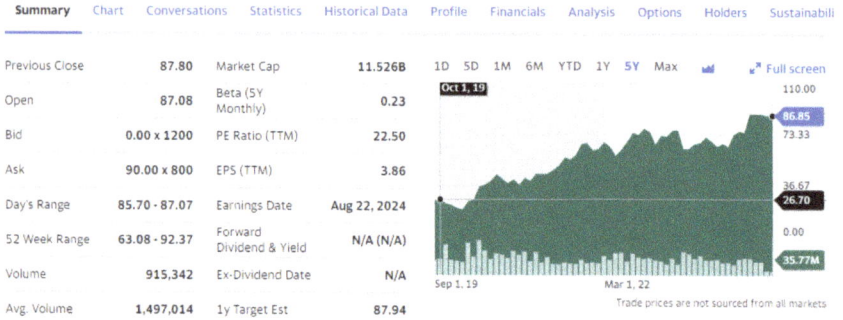

Summary | Chart | Conversations | Statistics | Historical Data | Profile | Financials | Analysis | Options | Holders | Sustainabili

Previous Close	87.80	Market Cap	11.526B
Open	87.08	Beta (5Y Monthly)	0.23
Bid	0.00 x 1200	PE Ratio (TTM)	22.50
Ask	90.00 x 800	EPS (TTM)	3.86
Day's Range	85.70 - 87.07	Earnings Date	Aug 22, 2024
52 Week Range	63.08 - 92.37	Forward Dividend & Yield	N/A (N/A)
Volume	915,342	Ex-Dividend Date	N/A
Avg. Volume	1,497,014	1y Target Est	87.94

Ameriprise Financial, Inc. (AMP)
NYSE - Nasdaq Real Time Price. Currency in USD
☆ Follow   👥 Visitors trend 2W ↑ 10W ↑ 9M ↑

402.61 -15.75 (-3.76%)   **403.33** +2.20 (+0.55%)
At close: August 2 04:00PM EDT   Pre-Market: 9:05AM EDT

$ Dividend   AMP announced a cash dividend of 1.48 with an ex-date of Aug. 5, 2024

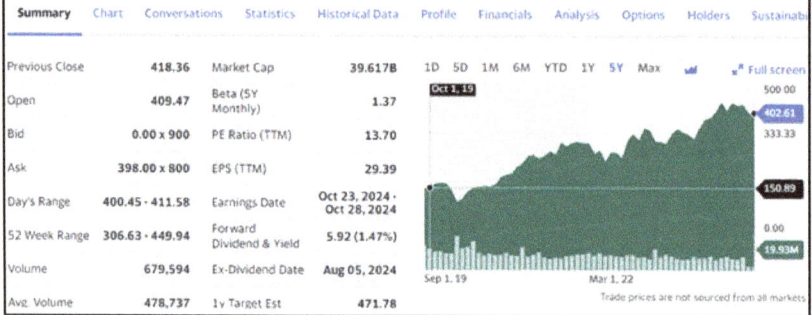

Summary | Chart | Conversations | Statistics | Historical Data | Profile | Financials | Analysis | Options | Holders | Sustainabi

Previous Close	418.36	Market Cap	39.617B
Open	409.47	Beta (5Y Monthly)	1.37
Bid	0.00 x 900	PE Ratio (TTM)	13.70
Ask	398.00 x 800	EPS (TTM)	29.39
Day's Range	400.45 - 411.58	Earnings Date	Oct 23, 2024 - Oct 28, 2024
52 Week Range	306.63 - 449.94	Forward Dividend & Yield	5.92 (1.47%)
Volume	679,594	Ex-Dividend Date	Aug 05, 2024
Avg. Volume	478,737	1y Target Est	471.78

Most Important Rule:
Invest in companies with a chart for the last five years similar to the one of Ameriprise Financial, Inc. It demonstrates a solid, unified approach to how the business is succeeding. Look for a unified culture with a winning mindset throughout the business.

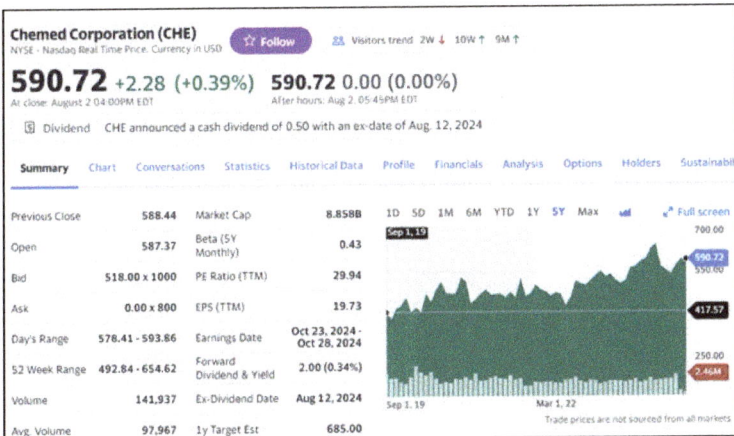

Chemed Corporation (CHE)
NYSE - Nasdaq Real Time Price. Currency in USD · ☆ Follow · 🔍 Visitors trend 2W ↓ 10W ↑ 9M ↑

590.72 +2.28 (+0.39%)   **590.72** 0.00 (0.00%)
At close: August 2 04:00PM EDT   After hours: Aug 2 05:45PM EDT

💲 Dividend   CHE announced a cash dividend of 0.50 with an ex-date of Aug. 12, 2024

Summary   Chart   Conversations   Statistics   Historical Data   Profile   Financials   Analysis   Options   Holders   Sustainabil

Previous Close	588.44	Market Cap	8.858B
Open	587.37	Beta (5Y Monthly)	0.43
Bid	518.00 x 1000	PE Ratio (TTM)	29.94
Ask	0.00 x 800	EPS (TTM)	19.73
Day's Range	578.41 - 593.86	Earnings Date	Oct 23, 2024 - Oct 28, 2024
52 Week Range	492.84 - 654.62	Forward Dividend & Yield	2.00 (0.34%)
Volume	141,937	Ex-Dividend Date	Aug 12, 2024
Avg. Volume	97,967	1y Target Est	685.00

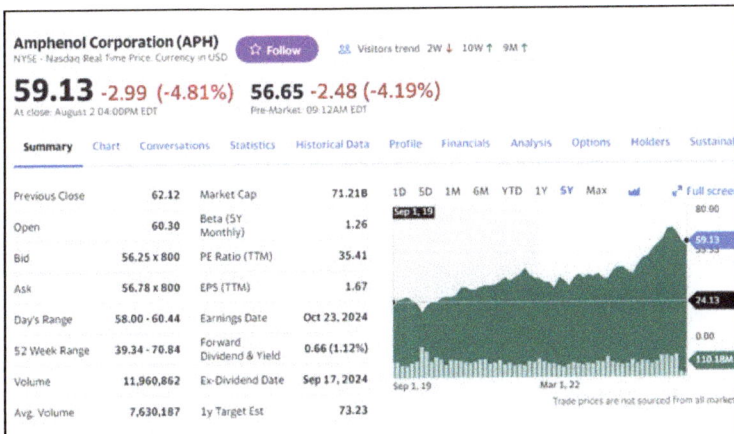

Amphenol Corporation (APH)
NYSE - Nasdaq Real Time Price. Currency in USD · ☆ Follow · 🔍 Visitors trend 2W ↓ 10W ↑ 9M ↑

59.13 -2.99 (-4.81%)   **56.65** -2.48 (-4.19%)
At close: August 2 04:00PM EDT   Pre-Market: 09:12AM EDT

Summary   Chart   Conversations   Statistics   Historical Data   Profile   Financials   Analysis   Options   Holders   Sustainab

Previous Close	62.12	Market Cap	71.21B
Open	60.30	Beta (5Y Monthly)	1.26
Bid	56.25 x 800	PE Ratio (TTM)	35.41
Ask	56.78 x 800	EPS (TTM)	1.67
Day's Range	58.00 - 60.44	Earnings Date	Oct 23, 2024
52 Week Range	39.34 - 70.84	Forward Dividend & Yield	0.66 (1.12%)
Volume	11,960,862	Ex-Dividend Date	Sep 17, 2024
Avg. Volume	7,630,187	1y Target Est	73.23

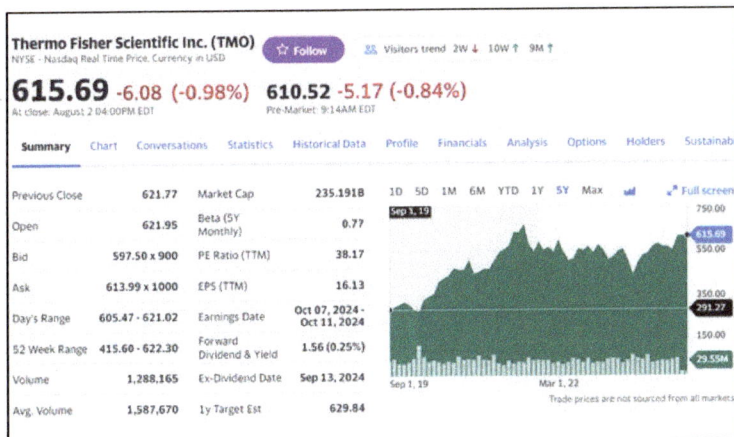

Thermo Fisher Scientific Inc. (TMO)
NYSE - Nasdaq Real Time Price. Currency in USD · ☆ Follow · 🔍 Visitors trend 2W ↓ 10W ↑ 9M ↑

615.69 -6.08 (-0.98%)   **610.52** -5.17 (-0.84%)
At close: August 2 04:00PM EDT   Pre-Market: 9:14AM EDT

Summary   Chart   Conversations   Statistics   Historical Data   Profile   Financials   Analysis   Options   Holders   Sustainabi

Previous Close	621.77	Market Cap	235.191B
Open	621.95	Beta (5Y Monthly)	0.77
Bid	597.50 x 900	PE Ratio (TTM)	38.17
Ask	613.99 x 1000	EPS (TTM)	16.13
Day's Range	605.47 - 621.02	Earnings Date	Oct 07, 2024 - Oct 11, 2024
52 Week Range	415.60 - 622.30	Forward Dividend & Yield	1.56 (0.25%)
Volume	1,288,165	Ex-Dividend Date	Sep 13, 2024
Avg. Volume	1,587,670	1y Target Est	629.84

You can go to *Finance.Yahoo.com* and look at the other stocks and those you like.

These are meant as suggestions to investigate but all have decent prospects over the long run. Will they double again in five years? We expect most of them will.

Apple, Microsoft, and Deere have also been long-term winners. Companies that have a dedicated product line and/or service with a culture that promotes innovative ideas, growth, and honorable business practices will reward investors year after year.

Investment Guideline 2

When choosing between two equally well-recommended companies, pick the one with the most valuable human capital. The companies doing well tody are high-tech and pharmaceutical. It's not by accident. Their employees add more value and are harder to replace.

Corollary: If you're in a hurry or can't decide, buy a highly rated Big Blue-Chip stock since they have developed a lot of human capital over the years.

Chapter 7

The Secret Art of Making Bread

In truth, making yeast bread is really easy, even for beginners. Learn a few simple rules and techniques and you will never again feel intimidated to try any type of bread or bread recipe. Bread is a matter of patience and a knowledgeable eye. There are no absolutes in the bread world, you must learn to think past numbers such as measurements and time and get straight to the factors that will ensure you have great bread every time.

— "Mamma" from *oldfashionedfamilies.com*

The same goes for picking stocks to buy. Develop a knowledgeable eye and don't overpay. Play your game, not their game. The best advice is to watch and wait. Be patient and let the stock come to you. Stocks are on sale every business day of the year. There is the fear of missing out, but with so many excellent companies, you can just keep looking. But you can't buy them all, so you settle on one. You're expecting to own at most a dozen stocks so wait until the time is right. It is much like baking bread. You need the right flour, fresh yeast, water, salt, and fat. With stocks you need money, recent analyst reports, instinct, and patience. There is no substitute for time and patience in the kitchen or the stock market.

The first similarity between stocks and bread is that you must give them time to rise. We know that sounds corny, but often when a stock goes up, you buy it, and then it plateaus. It can be a long time before a stock rises to the point where you actually make a decent amount of money. But the worst situation is when it goes down and languishes for an extended period.

As we write this, Altria stock is stuck in first gear. Altria is the domestic portion of the former Philip Morris Tobacco. Altria now has headquarters in Richmond, Virginia, in the former Reynolds Metals building just west of the city limits. It has many stable, well-run businesses, but its former CEO, Howard Willard, convinced the board to invest in Juul Labs, the maker of e-cigarettes in December 2018. Altria's 35% investment in Juul Labs soured in early 2020 causing Altria to write down its investment and replace its CEO. Because its businesses are mostly tobacco related, much of its sales are flat. However, the company can raise cigarette prices due to the addictive nature of the product.

The question is how good an investment is Altria? It is dough but not rising if you own it. It will never make the money it once did. Analysts say it's a very solid business, and it will likely continue to generate significant profits but not the growth that many other companies offer. It is dough that will not rise sufficiently to be baked and served with a meal. Sadly, we have invested in this company at times. Investments can sour or, in this case, not rise the way one would like. The cook doesn't throw away the dough that has been folded into loaves and needs only to rise to the required level to go into the oven. The redeeming quality of this investment is that it pays an unusually high dividend and provides grants to many not-for-profit organizations in Central Virginia and beyond.

The theme of this chapter is patience, planning, and then waiting some more. Warren Buffett said it best, "No matter how great the talent or efforts, some things just take time. You can't produce a baby in one month by getting nine women pregnant."

Cabotwealth.com spoke of patience when investing in a simple way:

> *The toughest thing in stock investing is to do nothing. That's right, nothing! Once you buy a stock and watch it move up, down and all around for a few weeks, there is an urge to take action. Since you bought the stock, you've probably read numerous investment news stories on the market in general and your stock in particular. And even if you are only watching your stock (as we advise), you've taken in many days of price, volume and relative performance action. With so much input, it's easy to have your thinking swayed, which creates temptation to take action.*

Another way to say it is that most investors lack patience. That's a shame because almost every successful investor we've ever met or read about has an abundance of patience. After all, if you're correct on a stock, what's the point of rushing things?

Our friend's model portfolio changed slowly over time. Some stocks rose faster than others, but they all went up. If we were happy with a stock's performance but felt it had risen as much as we could expect, we folded it like bread dough into another stock.

Suze Orman agrees. She writes,

> *People are always asking me what they should invest in, or whether they should buy Investment A or sell Investment B. There seems to be this sense that being actively involved is important. I am here to tell you that patience could be your most valuable investing skill. Especially when it comes to saving for retirement. Once you settle on the right mix of stocks and bonds for your portfolio, ... my advice is just focus on funneling as much money as possible into those portfolios.*

A Recipe for Sourdough Bread

Sourdough bread relies on a starter—a small amount of dough with yeast in it that is saved every time you make bread (most people freeze it). The yeast is, of course, the rising mechanism, or the agent of growth. In this recipe, your starter is an initial purchase of something...

- Buy a few shares of something (that you have researched, of course, and can afford)
- Adopt the specific goal for this stock of growing it (letting it rise) to a target price.
- Utilize the various types of yeast:
- Wait for a time when it is down and buy more shares.
- Use dividends to automatically reinvest in more stock.
- Buy a little more each month.
- Use windfall money to buy more shares.
- Use leftover proceeds from other transactions to buy more shares.
- By the time you have 100 shares, you will be shocked at how much your net has increased.
- The loaf of bread gets much bigger.

Patience Yields Profits

The owner of the portfolio we advised on at one point needed approximately $20,000, so she sold her Equinix holdings even though it incurred substantial tax liability. But the overall portfolio has continued to produce outsized gains even during the turbulence of the pandemic of 2020. Here is the portfolio after a substantial withdrawal but also after Apple declared a 4-for-1 stock split on Aug. 4, 2020.

Individual Brokerage -8297			Net Account Value $107,280.32			Total Unrealized Gain $80,471.37 (300.17%)			Day's Gain Unrealized $756.20 (0.71%)		› Sho
All Positions ⌄		› Filters	Customize	Edit Lots	Reset Sort						Wash sale
› Symbol	Actions		Last Price $	Change $	Change %	Qty #	Price Paid $	Day's Gain $	Total Gain $	Total Gain %	Value $ ▾
› AAPL ① ⚲	Trade ⌄	△ ⧉	438.66	2.91	0.67%	100	29.6743	291.00	40,891.15	1,374.56%	43,866.00
› AMZN ①	Trade ⌄	△ ⧉	3,138.83	26.94	0.87%	10	991.825	269.40	21,456.15	216.03%	31,388.30
› BABA ① ⚲	Trade ⌄	△ ⧉	262.20	4.26	1.65%	50	140.816	213.00	6,062.25	86.02%	13,110.00
› WIX ① ⚲	Trade ⌄	△ ⧉	304.55	2.02	0.67%	40	82.3429	80.80	8,881.33	269.08%	12,182.00
› DHI ① ⚲	Trade ⌄	△ ⧉	67.34	-0.96	-1.43%	100	35.4656	-96.00	3,180.49	89.50%	6,734.00
Cash Transfer money											$0.02
Total							$26,808.93	$756.20	$80,471.37	300.17%	$107,280.32

This portfolio has fewer stocks than we recommend, but with our friend's other holdings it makes sense not to sell any of these stocks. Several of them still have significant growth prospects for their future. Bear in mind, it took over ten years to put this together and reach the point of being able to harvest the portfolio for other purposes. Patience pays.

Investment Guideline 3

Don't invest in stocks for short-term gains. When asked what his holding period was for a stock, Warren Buffett said *forever*. A longer than three-year holding period allows management's strategy to demonstrate its efficacy. It helps an investor avoid the peaks and valleys of stock prices. Stocks, like bread, need to be left alone to rise. In most cases, if a stock doesn't rise after three years, it will likely be around the same price as when you bought it. Then decide if it needs more time or it's time to havest the funds and find another one.

Your portfolio tells a story. It is the story of a piece of your life where you went out on your own. Imagine early settlers going out to make their way. In early America, they headed west from Philadelphia, Boston, and Charleston into mostly woods. They cleared the land, built cabins and barns, raised livestock, and planted crops. Sometimes a crop failed, or the cow died. But they pressed on. Few of your investments will be roaring winners. You only need a few to succeed for you to succeed. Like any story, you don't know the ending until you get there. Is there any other choice but to go forward? On to the main course.

Life begins whenever you want it to begin.

—Sumner Redstone (1923-2020)

Chapter 8

Investing in America or Anywhere Else

Now, as a nation, we don't promise equal outcomes, but we were founded on the idea that everybody should have an equal opportunity to succeed. No matter who you are, what you look like, where you come from, you can make it. That's an essential promise of America. Where you start should not determine where you end up.

—President Barack Obama

America deserves and wants your input, your vision, your outcomes. It's an open economic door; no matter what people say or do. But you must lift your arm, grab the door knocker, and bring it down on the door plate. You must be determined and prepared to enter and take your place as an investor alongside people and institutions that own or control millions, even billions of dollars. Big wealth may have some advantages over you and me, but we can create smart, long-term strategies that greatly improve our results.

Most people want to save money, select an investment firm or financial adviser and then turn their money over to the firm they selected and wait for terrific results. Tradition and advertising paint a picture of well-groomed advisers making plans to match your life and help you succeed. To use an old saying, "Where are the customers' yachts?" We pay a significant percentage of our profits to these firms. You can do as well as the experts, equaling or exceeding the averages, but not every year. Some years the prices of the companies you invest in may not exceed the indices. You may have to give your stocks space to grow and time for longer-term initiatives to yield the returns you desire.

We sometimes forget our nation was built on the back of agriculture. America used to be just farms and land. Seasons, cycles, rain, markets, and cash made up the ingredients that allowed families to first survive and later to thrive. Compared to farming, the stock market is a picnic. Both the late Stephen Covey and Warren Buffett have referred to natural systems in their talks and in their personal actions. Stephen Covey asked an audience if anyone had ever crammed for an exam. Many raised their hands. Then he asked who had lived on a farm and a few people raised their hands. Then he asked who had ever "crammed" on a farm. There was laughter. You cannot grow tomatoes faster than the tomato plant is genetically able to do. And Buffett said, "No one buys a farm based on whether they think it's going to rain next year."

The stock market focuses daily on trends, news, and price actions. It's like the weather forecast. But the employees of businesses think about making better products, more effective medicines, improved software and faster semiconductor chips. They gather project teams and set objectives. The project team determines how long it will take to make a new product or improve an existing product. They are the farmers in the company whose stock you own. Most of them ignore the price of their company stock. They must focus on their work. The work of most companies cannot be rushed or speeded up. If Lockheed Martin receives an order for an F-35 fighter jet they know how long its production will take. They know how many jets they are currently obligated to build. They know the lead times of the companies that provide tires, wings, electronic components, and other parts. They can give the customer a fairly accurate time frame for producing a plane. If the Navy orders a new submarine, General Dynamics or Huntington Ingalls can provide a projected delivery time when they sign the contract. The Navy wants to maintain two suppliers capable of building submarines in case something happens to one supplier.

When you invest in a stock you cannot expect it to go up fifteen percent or any percent by Thanksgiving. In an interview with Becky Quick on CNBC on February 24, 2020, Warren Buffett said about buying stocks, "You're buying businesses." Because people can "make decisions every second with stocks," as opposed to investing in a physical entity like stores or farms, "they think an investment in stocks is different from an investment in a business. But it isn't." The first thing to think of before hitting the computer key to buy is to imagine you're signing a contract to buy the entire company and letting others run it for you. You must think like an owner first. Imagine you *are* Warren Buffett and buying a company that someone else will run for you. He warned investors in the same interview not to buy a stock just because you think it will go up in price. We said this before—there is a 50/50 chance the stock you buy on your first day of ownership will go down in price. Don't let that alarm you.

Why Is It a Good Idea To Buy Stocks in the First Place?

So why buy stocks to begin with? It's a fair question. When was the last time you had to drop off your car for a repair or check up? Are any of your appliances over twenty years old? How old is your television, your computer, your phone, your knee replacement? Not only do things wear out, but newer, improved models of those things sometimes require that you replace them. Economists have long said the simple fact is that human wants can never be satisfied so there will always be demand. For the stock market, it was often predicted that as people retired, Baby Boomers especially, and began to sell stocks, there would be more sellers than buyers so the market would go down in the twenty-first century. But even during the pandemic the stock market surged. There are many reasons for this. For one thing, companies have taken advantage of low interest rates to buy back the stock of their companies so every stock must be investigated individually. That's why we recommend investing in and monitoring individual stocks. Jim Cramer, the CNBC commentator and founder of *TheStreet.com*, said his philosophy is not to buy and hold but "buy and homework." You must follow what you own. Read about the companies you own. Think like Warren Buffett. "When you buy a share of stock you are buying the company." You are not posting a family picture on Facebook.

Every day you and your neighbors go to work either physically or remotely. You receive a paycheck that is used to pay for the things you already own or can use on additional purchases. You expect your income to keep growing, and it does. Companies create new and improved products that consumers desire. Also, companies can simply receive more money for the products they supply. Regulated utilities apply to raise the price of their product/service to maintain their allowable rates of return. Other companies such as hospitals raise prices as the costs of the drugs, procedures, tests, etc. rise. You want to invest in stocks to be on the receiving end of price increases if for no other reason. Money in a savings account will not rise more than the rate you agreed to when you opened the account. Sure, stocks have more risk and volatility, but they ultimately win almost every time. Stocks are not an opponent you want to have against you. You want to be in their corner.

Your government encourages and protects stockholders. The enormous bailouts of the great recession 2008-2009 saved the entire economy of the United States. It is *expected* that the government will intercede during times of economic crisis. This fact maintains the faith of Americans in their future and, hence, the future of the stock market. The government protects intellectual property rights so that companies will invest in new products that can be patented. Our economy exists in a virtual cocoon of protection, laws and regulations, courts, financial oversight of corporations, and maintenance of our money supply. We have a patent and trademark registry to protect innovation. The vast defense complex that oversees the nation ultimately enables businesses to open safely. Of course, as taxpayers, we pay for these protections. But since they exist shouldn't you invest to reap the benefits you are already required to pay for? Buy stocks and hold them for as long as we have a government based on freedom and property rights. From the website of *azcentral.com*, a website of Arizona Central Newspaper owned by Gannett Newspapers:

- Once upon a time, we thought child labor was OK. Now we see it as abusive and a place for government intervention. So, it is illegal.

- Over the last hundred years, in particular, the government's role in the market has expanded dramatically, initially to provide some regulation and framework to facilitate transactions across state lines.

- Later, the government created tools to finance the country's rapid expansion and participation in wars, including credit and loan guarantees for agricultural development, electrification, and home buying.

- It created tools to eliminate some of the shocks that come from the boom-and-bust cycles of all kinds of businesses, such as deposit insurance and unemployment. It also created tools to oversee the increasing complexity and sophistication of modern enterprise, including securities and banking regulation, and food and drug safety.

- Our nation, at every level, strives for constant improvement. The Japanese term *kaizen* refers to the concept of improving business activities to continuously elevate all functions and involve all employees from the CEO to the assembly line workers. It is a total company concept, but we argue that our entire nation focuses on kaizen. The stock market reflects this concept of kaizen across industries, government, healthcare, and markets.

But no government entity protects us from our own mistakes, so that's why we suggest you become adept at reading about companies before you invest in them and then follow their actions as they continue to grow and evolve. Oversight of financial reporting exists so the stock market has been made as safe as humanly possible.

The American Dream Is Not Dead Nor Does It Sleep

The dreams of every person in America, regardless of size, still exist. But we do not wish to give the impression that there are no problems in the United States. We recognize that major challenges exist deep within our nation. Instead, we want to emphasize that our nation has an attitude toward facing problems, creating solutions, and implementing those solutions to overcome adversity. This is also what companies do every day. We encourage you to adopt this can-do attitude as you plan your investments. We believe that America's infrastructure is behind the times. Some might even say our roads and airports are shoddy and not worthy of the greatest nation on the planet. Nature provided America with a landscape beyond compare, but to see that beauty requires airports, railroads, and highways. Every time maintenance of a road is deferred, it raises the cost of the future replacement. One day soon the American public will demand that the nation's infrastructure be brought up to the standards of other countries. This will lead to opportunities for companies that provide products and services to make these improvements. Some of those companies are:

- AECOM (ACM) - Engineering/Construction
- Jacobs Engineering Group (J) - Engineering/Construction
- Construction Partners (ROAD) - Engineering/Construction
- United Rentals (URI) - Machinery/Equipment
- H & E Equipment (HEES) - Machinery/Equipment
- Terex Corp (TEX) - Machinery/Equipment
- Oshkosh (OSH) - Machinery/Equipment
- Cemex (CX) - Concrete/Cement
- Vulcan Materials (VMC) - Concrete/Cement
- Martin Marietta Materials (MLM) - Concrete/Cement

Many of these companies should be on your watchlist for when rebuilding America comes to the forefront of the nation's projects. We will include some of these in our Pantry Stocks chapter.

The Wisdom Literature, some of us call *The Holy Bible*, says in Jeremiah 29:11, "'For I know the plans I have for you,' declares the Lord, 'plans to prosper you and not to harm you, plans to give you hope and a future.'" Dreams are not just the images that we have in sleep but can be the visions in our waking brains. Ralph Waldo Emerson said, "Do not follow where the path may lead. Go instead where there is no path and leave a trail." Investing provides the best dream opportunity most of us will ever see. A new day that you create may be just around the corner. There is no exact pre-built trail for you to follow. Each path, each portfolio, is different, unique, one of a kind. But you can also buy mutual funds, and they provide as good a return as any that we can suggest. What we're describing is booking your own airline and hotel, and taking a bike trip in Europe, stopping where you wish. Mutual Funds are more like taking a guided tour. It depends on your personality. Try the independent path first, we suggest. You can always switch to a travel agent for your next trip.

Playing the Game

Investment Guideline 4

"Play your game, don't play their game," a friend, Mark Y, said about how he manages his portfolio. Don't be driven out of your position if the market goes down precipitously. We've made that mistake too often and lost over and over. Think of yourself as an artist. Stocks are your paint pallette.

We don't want to imply that investing is not serious business, but it is *not* a competition. We can't help but compare our portfolios to the primary indices when they are displayed prominently above our portfolio. It's difficult to beat the Dow Jones Industrial Average or NASDAQ or S&P averages yearly and impossible to beat them daily. Over the years, you can often accomplish the feat, but no one says you must even look. Mutual funds use the indices as a guideline to show their clients how well they are doing. Since you're your only client, you can just skip this step. Measure you against you. Your only goal is to have more money than when you started and continue to make good choices.

It's easy to get caught up in the wild trashing of economic news, government data, media opinions, company-specific statements, earnings reports and all the advertisements from firms that want your attention and your investment dollars. *Investopedia.com* says, "When you buy a stock, you are purchasing a proportional share of an entire future stream of earnings. That's the reason for the valuation multiple: it is the price you are willing to pay for the future stream of earnings." For example, over the last ten years, our friend's investment in Apple rose tenfold—what's called a ten-bagger. Apple's earnings, new products, and overall image rose during those years despite the passing of Steve Jobs in 2011. Over the last ten years, Apple's stock price fluctuated, but our advice to our friend was to ignore these price declines.

Because of a 7-for-1 stock split on June 9, 2014, price charts flattened out. Our advice is to ignore, to the degree you can bear it, stock price fluctuations of the stocks you own.

The primary drivers of stock prices are mutual funds, individuals, fiduciaries of various stripes, foreign investors, and companies themselves. Companies buy up their own stock and sometimes the stock of companies they might acquire an interest in. For example, Berkshire Hathaway acquires stakes in companies as an investment. They own stakes in banks and until 2020, airlines, without owning the entire company. As an individual owning 100 shares or less of a stock, when you place an order, you are a price taker. It makes little sense to concern yourself with a stock price, in the grand scheme of things, for a small purchase.

What you will do is purchase stock and monitor it. If you decide that a stock you own remains a good investment, you will buy more of it when you have additional funds. You can call this strategy anything you wish. It used to be called a buy-and-hold strategy. Jim Cramer calls it a buy-and-homework strategy. The bottom line is to give your stocks enough time and distance to prove themselves. Depending on your life, imagine the holding period to match the length of time you own your home. Granted, some people buy houses, fix them up, and flip them within a year, but we recommend keeping your stock at least as long as you keep your car to give you a chance to see how it performs. A stock is not a vacation spot where you visit for a short time then leave and go back home.

Build Your Portfolio Like Decorating a Holiday Tree

This is simply another way of explaining how to build your portfolio. After you select the location of the tree—hallway, entrance foyer, family room—this is the same as selecting the bank or broker that will hold your portfolio. Prior to the internet and dynamic online databases, brokers mailed certificates to your home, or you picked them up from the broker. They were beautiful with gilding around the edges. You would have to rent a deposit box at the bank to keep them. But it was an era when investors expected to buy and hold stocks for a long time. It was not unusual to settle the estate of an elderly relative and find a fistful of gilt certificates in a lockbox. They, of course, cashed the dividend checks during all the years they held the stock. It was a different mindset. Plus, the activities of the companies changed slowly so holding their certificates was not unusual. Today, companies get bought out and merge more rapidly so issuing all those certificates would be impossibly cumbersome in today's faster paced investing world. You can see examples of stock certificates online. The Walt Disney Company stock certificate had not only a picture of Walt Disney but of some of the animated characters on it. Today, of course, your shares are electronic entries and can be bought and sold in a few seconds. In the past, the certificate had to be taken from your lockbox down to the broker's office and signed (and sometimes witnessed). It was then sent to the offices of the company to be retired so that the new owner's certificate could be issued.

After the tree is standing in the best location, the first thing to do is to establish a foundation—put on the lights. These lights circle the tree and can be seen from across the room. Depending on how many kinds of lights you use, these are the ones you will see every day, your largest monetary investment. When you set up your portfolio you want your first stock(s) to be companies that customers use every day. For example, one of your first stocks—one you won't ever sell or not sell for many years to come—would be a stock like Walmart, Kroger, your bank, or your local utility. These are the companies that consumers need every day. Then you begin with large decorations. These represent large and growing companies, leaders and innovators in the areas where they do business, including companies like Microsoft, Adobe, Target, and defense contractors (Lockheed-Martin, General Dynamics, and Huntington Ingalls.) While with real trees you might select similar decorations and group them, for a portfolio you want stocks in different industries. The next layer consists of smaller decorations. These are faster growing and innovative companies.

On the outer level many people add ribbons to their trees. These represent small pharmaceutical companies developing drugs for rare diseases or simply smaller pharma companies. Examples are Sarepta Therapeutics, Jazz Pharma, and BioMarin. Finally, you need a stunning tree topper. This could be a stock you investigated that has something unique going for it. Stocks that come to mind with some unique characteristics might be Penn National Gaming (online betting), CyberArk (security software), or Marvel Technologies (5G semiconductors.)

Your portfolio must have a variety of stocks to be truly diversified. Keep a picture of a holiday tree nearby as you think about building your portfolio if that helps your thinking process. It's a unique adventure, and the memory will stay with you for a long time.

Your Portfolio Will Change over Time

At first, we did not think we would be writing a book such as this, so we don't have screenshots of all the changes that go with our friend's successful portfolio. But Berkshire Hathaway has put online their annual letter to stockholders, which records their stock holdings at the end of each year. Bear in mind that many of the investments they hold and that generate sizable revenues and income are wholly owned. Therefore, this list includes only the companies they hold shares of, not all the companies they own and have folded into their corporate structure.

Berkshire Hathaway
Year-end 2000 (list of those held valued more than $1billion)

		12/31/00	
		Cost	*Market*
Shares	*Company*	(dollars in millions)	
151,610,700	American Express Company	$1,470	$ 8,329
200,000,000	The Coca-Cola Company	1,299	12,188
96,000,000	The Gillette Company	600	3,468
1,727,765	The Washington Post Company	11	1,066
55,071,380	Wells Fargo & Company	319	3,067
	Others	6,703	9,501
	Total Common Stocks	$10,402	$ 37,619

Berkshire Hathaway
Year-end 2010

		12/31/10		
		Percentage of Company Owned	*Cost **	*Market*
Shares	*Company*		(in millions)	
151,610,700	American Express Company	12.6	$ 1,287	$ 6,507
225,000,000	BYD Company, Ltd.	9.9	232	1,182
200,000,000	The Coca-Cola Company	8.6	1,299	13,154
29,109,637	ConocoPhillips	2.0	2,028	1,982
45,022,563	Johnson & Johnson	1.6	2,749	2,785
97,214,584	Kraft Foods Inc.	5.6	3,207	3,063
19,259,600	Munich Re	10.5	2,896	2,924
3,947,555	POSCO	4.6	768	1,706
72,391,036	The Procter & Gamble Company	2.6	464	4,657
25,848,838	Sanofi-Aventis	2.0	2,060	1,656
242,163,773	Tesco plc	3.0	1,414	1,608
78,060,769	U.S. Bancorp	4.1	2,401	2,105
39,037,142	Wal-Mart Stores, Inc.	1.1	1,893	2,105
358,936,125	Wells Fargo & Company	6.8	8,015	11,123
	Others		3,020	4,956
	Total Common Stocks Carried at Market		$33,733	$61,513

Berkshire Hathaway
Year-end 2019 (15 with the largest market value)

Shares*	Company	Percentage of Company Owned	12/31/19 Cost**	Market
			(in millions)	
151,610,700	American Express Company	18.7	$ 1,287	$ 18,874
250,866,566	Apple Inc.	5.7	35,287	73,667
947,760,000	Bank of America Corp.	10.7	12,560	33,380
81,488,751	The Bank of New York Mellon Corp.	9.0	3,696	4,101
5,426,609	Charter Communications, Inc.	2.6	944	2,632
400,000,000	The Coca-Cola Company	9.3	1,299	22,140
70,910,456	Delta Air Lines, Inc.	11.0	3,125	4,147
12,435,814	The Goldman Sachs Group, Inc.	3.5	890	2,859
60,059,932	JPMorgan Chase & Co.	1.9	6,556	8,372
24,669,778	Moody's Corporation	13.1	248	5,857
46,692,713	Southwest Airlines Co.	9.0	1,940	2,520
21,938,642	United Continental Holdings Inc.	8.7	1,195	1,933
149,497,786	U.S. Bancorp	9.7	5,709	8,864
10,239,160	Visa Inc.	0.6	349	1,924
345,688,918	Wells Fargo & Company	8.4	7,040	18,598
	Others***		28,215	38,159
	Total Equity Investments Carried at Market		$110,340	$248,027

* Excludes shares held by pension funds of Berkshire subsidiaries.
** This is our actual purchase price and also our tax basis.
*** Includes $10 billion investment in Occidental Petroleum Corporation consisting of preferred stock and warrants to buy common stock.

It would be beneficial to read some of Berkshire Hathaway's letters to stockholders. You can discover how they built their portfolio. Consider them free lessons. You can search the internet for these letters, which are also available in a book.

Notice that some of the investments are retained year after year. American Express and Coca-Cola have been in this portfolio for decades. Inflation has a subtle effect on the stock price because the purchase price will never change, but the current value will generally rise due both to the growth of the company and, to a lesser extent, inflation. The lesson is that if a few stocks do extraordinarily well, then you simply keep them year after year. In the case of Berkshire Hathaway, they book ever-increasing dividends. These annual reports are a roadmap for building a portfolio. Grow slowly with patience. Notice how the value of Berkshire-Hathaway goes exponential as time goes by. Yours will too. Just keep working your plan. If you are young, time is on your side. All you must do is marry your older self to your younger self and let the older you run your stock portfolio. Simply emulate the actions of Warren Buffett—admit and learn from your mistakes and then build a solid portfolio. Money is being made across our country. But you must invest yourself in it.

Berkshire Hathaway started in 1965, an outgrowth from Buffett Partnership, Ltd. that he created in 1956. Over sixty-four years the company grew to own sixty subsidiary companies plus shares in many other companies. These holdings can be found on the company's website. So, not only did Buffett and Charlie Munger decide which companies to hold the stock of, they also had to select companies and managers of other companies when they purchased them outright. It's enough for most of us just to sort through potential investments without having to select managers as well.

Peter Lynch's Guidelines To Being Successful

(From *One Up on Wall Street*)

- Sometime in the next month, year, or three years, the market will decline sharply.
- Market declines are great opportunities to buy stocks in companies you like.
- Corrections—stocks going down a lot—push great stocks down to bargain prices.
- Trying to predict the market over any period is impossible.
- You don't have to be right all the time, just a few times will make you a winner.
- It takes years, not months, to produce big results.
- You can also make your gains through a series of 20-30 percent gains in stalwarts.
- Stock prices often move in opposite directions from fundamentals, but in the end sustained profits will prevail and drive prices higher.
- Just because a company is doing poorly doesn't mean it can't do worse!
- Just because the price goes down doesn't mean you're wrong to invest in a stock.
- A stock does not know that you own it.
- When you find a favorable stock or get a great earnings report, add to your holdings.

- You don't improve results by pulling out the flowers and watering the weeds.

- If you don't think you can beat the market, then buy mutual funds and save yourself a lot of extra work and money.

- It's okay to miss some great stocks and still beat the market.

Summary

What if a million people took up the concepts of this book, and over time each one developed a portfolio of $10,000? After a few decades, smaller investors could then own billions of dollars of stocks. There is an abundance of opportunities, and entrepreneurs create new ones all the time. You only have to hold out your hand and keep an open mind to acquire superior investments. But you must stand your ground when the market says to drop all your stocks and run away. Stand on the mound and keep pitching even if it's raining.

Chapter 9

What Could Possibly Go Wrong?

When the dog bites, when the bee stings, when I'm feeling sad
I simply remember my favorite things, and then I don't feel so bad.

—Julie Andrews / *The Sound of Music*

When your stocks go down, when the bee stings, when I'm feeling sad, I simply remember my favorite things, and then I don't feel so bad.

—our lyrics for this song

If they like you, they kill you last.

—old Wall Street saying

Most of the commentators that want your money use *extreme* examples, both good and bad. Robert Schiller of Yale University has a video that shows a chart demonstrating that the stock market moves very little 99% of the time. But we concentrate on the extremes as if they happen frequently. Look how much the world focused on *Titanic*—for over a century. There's been nothing like it since. The COVID-19 Pandemic in our country deserves to have tribunals set up and politicians grilled like sea captains who lost their ships! Many citizens and neighbors refused to wear masks or avoid large public gatherings, ignoring the advice of medical professionals. How you act during market extremes reflects your preparation and mental training. Please expect some of your stocks to go down for no reason at all. The price swings that take place for any given stock are out of your control.

Too often, it feels like you're in a tennis match with the market. You cannot get your racket on the ball time after time. The market, what feels like your opponent, keeps winning and running up the score. You lose money every day. That's called character building. You do research to see if there is something fundamentally wrong with either your stocks or the economic environment. But most of the time, top athletes, after they lose, return to training and fundamentals. If you get discouraged, read quotes by someone like Vince Lombardi (Coach of the Green Bay Packers in the 1960s):

> *Success is like anything worthwhile. It has a price. You have to pay the price to win, and you have to pay the price to get to the point where success is possible. Most importantly, you must pay the price to stay there.*
>
> *Perfection is not attainable. But if we chase perfection, we can catch excellence.*
>
> *The only place success comes before work is in the dictionary.*

There are always problems or difficulties at the extremes. Many people were shaken by the March 2020 COVID-19 market decline. How do you handle it when things go wrong? COVID arguably took away many of the important day-to-day decisions people were making as a matter of routine. Financial crises and political uncertainty can make managing your own stock account take on a completely different nature. But remember, you are the driver of the bus, do not allow the market to drive your decisions. Don't detour until you can no longer see a path forward. Think of financial opportunities as airports of different sizes, locations, and length of runway. When a crisis comes, it is not a matter of bailing out as much as finding the right airport to land or take off from.

Regret has no place in your new investor mindset. You can learn from mistakes, but you can't let them hinder your future decision-making or crowd out your imagination.

> *Pain is inevitable, suffering is optional.*
> —the Dalai Lama

> *How to make a million on Wall Street? Start with two million.*
> —an old joke on Wall Street

Suppose you've saved and invested as we suggest and have established a portfolio worth $10,000 over six years. Along comes another new virus, and because of panic selling, the next day your portfolio is worth $7,000. What will you do? What will happen to you? Will your spouse leave you? Will your children go hungry? Do you have some other funds available to you? This scenario may occur several times during your investment life. After 9/11, the market went down. Always be prepared. But do not panic. Either get into the lifeboat or decide to ride out the storm. The Great Depression of the 1930s was the longest downtime, lasting about fifteen years, so these unexpected circumstances can be painful, but they always end.

On YouTube you will find a series of videos called "Restoration Home," featuring primarily British couples who purchase derelict structures with the plan to make them into their homes. They plan, set aside money, and even quit their jobs to make their dreams come true. There are always difficulties that are too numerous and unique to list, but the shows conclude with a happy ending. Problems almost always have a solution if you're willing to work hard enough.

If that doesn't lift your spirits, listen to James Horner's music from the *Field of Dreams* Soundtrack, especially, "The Place Where Dreams Come True." You can watch the movie too and many others for inspiration. A lyric by Oscar Hammerstein in a song from *South Pacific* says, "if you don't have a dream, how you gonna have a dream come true?"

Everyone loses some money, but not all, at some time in the stock market. But if you look at graphs of the market, a rising tide does indeed lift all boats. That's why, for emphasis, diversification across industries is important. It's the only thing that will save you. Imagine if the White Star line had built ten separate ships to carry the same 2,224 passengers and crew that were on *Titanic*. It's doubtful all ten would have sunk. If you own a boat of whatever size, rename it *The Diversification*. Then sail on.

Historic Example of Loss
Black Monday—October 13, 1987

On that day the stock market went crazy. You can read about it for yourself. Anything can happen. From August 1982 to August 1987, the Dow Jones Industrial Average rose from 776 to 2,722. On Monday, October 18,1987, the market took a precipitous fall of 508 points or 22.6 percent. In a situation like that, one tends to lose all sense of calm. Our reaction was to try to end the pain. Selling at a loss seemed the only response. Years later, Warren Buffet said he made a different assessment. He acted with calm reassurance. He did nothing. The only move when you know that the stocks you own will likely recover in time is to do nothing, but it's the hardest thing to do. Being young and inexperienced, we panicked, selling at a terrible loss. The only good news was that our portfolio was not large. The Dow recovered most of its losses within a short time.

Another Example—the Internet Bubble in 2000

Those who are old enough to remember the late 1990s and early 2000s remember the "Wild West" days of the internet and the beginnings of the WWW (World-Wide-Web). It created amazing resources and connections but also trash and viruses. Sometimes one organization could fall victim to those things at the same time.

Students using the web were taught to check the source, and then check the source of the source, and evaluate that for veracity. The same rules still apply. The wealth of information is both a blessing and a curse, and while we are advising you to utilize available online sources, the old Wild-West warning from years ago still applies.

Never transfer money online except through your own verified financial institution or a reputable online broker. And always check on the site or organization you are relying on. Use caution with email, as it can easily be accessed by those with ill intentions.

Brokers, Money Managers and Those With a System For Beating the Market

The goal of professionals providing investment advice is to accumulate as much in assets under management (AUM) as possible. That way they can collect fees from your account or transactions. If you have a ten-thousand-dollar account, they buy and sell assets in that account along with thousands of others. During the process they also charge you for the expenses, *and* you still bear the risk they are taking on your behalf. We are promoting the idea instead that you are the cook in the kitchen, and you can equip yourself to manage some of the risk, some of the research and *all* of the satisfaction that comes with doing something yourself that leads to positive economic outcomes.

What can possibly go wrong?

- The market can dip due to a sudden, unexpected crisis.
- A large fund can struggle and suppress or threaten the market (ex. Long Term Capital).
- New technology can render old standbys suddenly obsolete.

- A scandal can upset the organizational stability of a company (including leadership changes. For example, when Lee Iacocca took over Chrysler).

- Favorite stocks can crash and make you worry about others that are fine.

- A bad day or a bad week on the market can shake your confidence disproportionately.

- Pharmaceutical companies have drugs that fail.

- Politicians can interfere in the markets with laws they float on the media.

- External powers can drive companies out of business (OPEC for instance).

- A small stock that you just bought on advice immediately declines.

But these factors are already built into the system. You simply must ride it out. You must diversify and stick to the plan.

Some Guidelines To Keep in Mind during Downturns

Reality struck our stocks on August 17, 2024. The stocks that had been rising, like those in Artificial Intelligence entities, fell a lot. In other words, money managers got spooked by headlines about potential tariffs, and those who traded short stocks borrowed shares and sold them, expecting that they would decline, causing tremendous selling pressure. Everyone rushed to the exits all at once. Fortunately, regulations put in place over the years relieved some of the selling pressure and kept things operating smoothly. This is a topic you should research on your own. But here's what happened. Stocks such as Nvidia, Micron Technology, and Super Micro Computers that are in our portfolio fell around six percent. Plus, anything related to that also got sold. We owned Modine Manufacturing of Racine, Wisconsin, a company we had stumbled on by chance. Demand for heat exchange products had soared because of potential data center construction. Artificial Intelligence computing generates lots of heat. On that day, Modine hit a high of $116.48 in the morning and closed at $106.48 at the end of trading. But our cost basis meant we could sit tight. At the close, declines put those stocks in the account related to AI into a loss position. Because we're in this for the long run, we did not sell. Market swings are built into the market. Prepare for them mentally and financially. It's okay to sell, but remember if you do, you cannot buy it back for thirty days or your trade will be considered a "wash sale" and you will lose the option to declare the loss on your taxes. We know this for certain:

- The price of a stock can go down for no reason.

- Don't buy a stock solely because it has fallen a lot.

- Don't abandon your stock(s) because they have fallen a lot.

> **What to Remember when Your Stock Declines**
> Many years ago, when oil drilling stocks were not just flattened, but in the toilet, the CEO of Rowan Drilling (merged into something else now) said, I am reminded of what we say in West Texas during a drought. Every day we are one day closer to rain. That may be a small comfort in most situations, but every stock that declines is working to bounce back one day at a time.

On the plus side, infrastructure and consumer products are generally not built to last forever, and there are some services and products that will present constant opportunities to invest. The theory of capitalism itself is predicated on continuous long-term growth. Human desires can never be satisfied.

Referring to the earlier chapter on psychology, it is often possible that you only think—or more importantly—feel something has gone terribly wrong. Part of retraining the brain to be in the stock market "kitchen" is preparing for things that turn out with question marks. Why didn't that cake rise? Why is the chicken still undercooked in the center? Why did the broth turn this color? These surprises will inevitably happen to your investments. In the same way, chefs who practice and innovate make fewer mistakes and encounter fewer surprises the longer they ply their trade. The stock market kitchen works the same way.

You may be thinking, "This is easy for you to say. It's *my* money, not yours, that might be at risk." As difficult as it is to acknowledge, that is your old brain resisting this new perspective. Yes, in a technical sense, it is your real money at risk—you should never prioritize risking money in the market over meeting life's basic needs. But it is money you are using to make more money; it is a set of ingredients with which you make a conscious decision to cook something.

> **Investment Guideline 5**
> Be grateful you were able to save some money to participate in the greatest economy with the most opportunities for future gains. It will get better from wherever your stocks are at this moment. Consumers' wants can never be satisfied; that's why they will return again and again to purchase cars, clothes, Christmas gifts, and computers. You won't go broke with a diversified portfolio. It just sometimes feels that way!

Markets Can Decline for No Reason at All

On September 3, 2020, the stock market suddenly got hit. It started to fall from the opening bell then continued for the rest of the day. Almost all stocks declined that day. Even stocks that had not risen briskly in the summer of 2020 got hit, though not as much.

Our friend's monitored portfolio at market close 9-3-2020:

Individual Brokerage -8297			Net Account Value $114,162.52		Total Unrealized Gain $87,254.07 (325.47%)		Day's Gain Unrealized -$7,782.40 (-6.39%)		› Show more

All Positions ⌄ › Filters Customize Edit Lots Reset Sort   Wash sale adjust

⟩ Symbol	Actions		Last Price $	Change $	Change %	Qty #	Price Paid $	Day's Gain $	Total Gain $	Total Gain %	Value $ ▾
› AAPL ⓘ	Trade ⌄	⌂ ☰	120.88	-10.52	-8.01%	400	7.4186	-4,208.00	45,377.16	1,525.36%	48,352.00
› AMZN ⓘ	Trade ⌄	⌂ ☰	3,368.00	-163.45	-4.63%	10	991.825	-1,634.50	23,747.85	239.10%	33,680.00
› BABA ⓘ	Trade ⌄	⌂ ☰	282.50	-13.57	-4.58%	50	140.816	-678.50	7,077.25	100.42%	14,125.00
› WIX ⓘ	Trade ⌄	⌂ ☰	271.25	-25.71	-8.66%	40	82.3429	-1,028.40	7,549.33	228.72%	10,850.00
› DHI ⓘ	Trade ⌄	⌂ ☰	70.56	-2.33	-3.20%	100	35.4656	-233.00	3,502.49	98.56%	7,056.00
Cash Transfer money											$99.52
Total							$26,808.93	-$7,782.40	$87,254.07	325.47%	$114,162.52

This happens often so it's important not to panic.

Chapter 10

Examples of Stock Recipes

A recipe [portfolio] has no soul. You as the cook must bring soul to the recipe.
—Thomas Keller, author of *The French Laundry* cookbook

The best chefs ultimately invent their own recipes. In this chapter you will find examples of groups of companies recommended by investment advisers. We are not endorsing any of them, but some will achieve superior results. Now that you have some knowledge under your belt, it's time to explore your personal goals, traits, and interests that enable you to create your own unique recipes. To be a master chef (or investor) you will want to come up with some of your own ideas. You can examine other recipes and pick some for your own portfolio.

Let's revisit some key ideas. First, make sure you are learning how to cook in your kitchen. To think like a cook (an investor), you must be surrounded by all the resources you need—pans, ovens, cookbooks, ingredients—but you also need a consistent space where you are able to practice your skills and learn new techniques. Jack's wife reads cookbooks in bed before she goes to sleep, which is clever. It's a calm, quiet place—consistent night after night—where she can deeply-process information, think creatively away from the day's stresses, and focus on cooking within the bigger world of cuisine. It is the last thing her brain processes before she goes to sleep.

For an investor, we recommend finding a place that you can use most of the time, a place that is relatively limited by distractions, not connected with the stress of work, and has access to any technology you might need. It is important that you develop the right habits to help you think like an investor (a chef). A coffee shop is great, especially if it is the same one every time and you always go at the same time of day. Obviously, no one can keep to a perfect monk-like schedule, but the more routine you can build into your training, the more results you will see in your portfolio. You wouldn't try to cook an elaborate meal in your bathroom, or basement (I hope), so don't try to train yourself as an investor in the wrong space.

You've probably heard fantastic stories of people who have hit it rich following a hunch, made their millions, and retired. To reiterate a key point, be wary of basing decisions solely on hunches, guesses, or feelings. Many people have advanced inductive skills that seem like gifts, but they are actually showing on the outside a deep, sometimes subconscious, process that has been taking place on the inside—filled with mountains of information that their brains constantly take in and organize, even when they are busy with other distractions. Look at Malcolm Gladwell's *Blink*. Instead of playing hunches, we recommend you replace hunch with "*hanch*."

Hanch—Ways To Find, Explore, and Follow Stocks

- Hundred-year-old companies may not be the best investment option; try to go with newer companies that may carry less baggage. But remain flexible.

- Analysts can provide so much more insight than we can alone; rely on a healthy dose of their expertise.

- News is like salt—use it every day in every recipe, but sparingly; stay alert to company and economic events as much as you can without allowing it to derail your portfolio.

- Consistency is a hallmark of logical thinking; try not to break your own rules.

- Heterogeneity or "medley cooking" is a mix; always diversify on several levels like adding spinach to a dish.

Solid Growers—Government Contractors

These companies will likely neither soar nor collapse. Their main income comes from government contracts. They sometimes stay at the same prices for years but almost always show an increase for a three-year period.

- L3Harris Technologies (LHX)
- Northrup Grumman (NOC)
- General Dynamics (GD)
- Lockheed Martin (LMT)
- Leidos Holdings (LDOS)
- Huntington Ingalls Industries (HII)

Never buy a lot of these, but a few are solid additions to any portfolio.

The Windfall Appetizer

Start out with any small windfall you receive (like birthday or graduation gifts, or Jack sometimes receives a small honorarium for a presentation or talk, for example):

- Add it immediately to your investment account such as with E*TRADE.
- Find a medium-priced stock in a new emergent technology.
- Buy the handful of shares your cash allows.
- Place the funds in the freezer and leave alone.

Good cooks like to use fresh ingredients like fresh vegetables or herbs from their own backyard. Don't fail to delimit your news overload by Googling the state or region you live in, and "publicly held companies." You will be surprised at what is in your own backyard. This gives you a smaller news cycle to look at, and there may even be cases where you can visit the business in person to ask for investor information. Charles Payne simply recommends that you consider buying stock in companies you purchase things from all the time.

Good Companies that Might Be "Safer" Investments

The stock market is filled with solid companies that are less volatile, have increased in price slowly, and pay dividends. When they appear on your investment radar, they may make a good addition to your portfolio because they demand less attention. Here are some to evaluate:

- Allison Transmission Holdings, Inc. (ALSN)

This stock is a foundational component in the transportation industry. It is the world's largest manufacturer of fully automatic transmissions for medium- and heavy-duty commercial vehicles, US military vehicles, and hybrid propulsion systems for transit buses. Demand for many of its products arises from slow-growing markets. It's likely there will not be a surge in demand for bus transmissions. The company's roots trace back to 1912. Because of its age, we would not recommend buying this company, but there are similar companies that operate with up-to-date methods and equipment. Merrill Lynch sees its price rising over the next few years, and its dividend will likely rise a little. So, if you're uncertain about an investment in technology and may need the money in a few years, this company or one like it may fit your profile. Stocks are like suits on a rack in a store. Some styles work for special occasions.

Some Stocks Recommended on *Finance.Yahoo.com*

A good time to visit this page is on Sunday. When the flow of finance news is low, writers post lists/recipes from analysts and investment institutions. They usually erect "umbrellas," gathering similar stocks such as healthcare, high dividend, semiconductor, or 5G companies, airlines or Chinese companies. An example of dividend recommendations is from TipRanks, who list their highest rated stocks:

- AT&T, Inc. (symbol T) recommended by Ivan Feinseth, a 5-star analyst with Tigress Financial

- Physicians Realty Trust (symbol DOC) recommended by Craig Kucera from B. Riley Financial, Inc.

- LyondellBasell (symbol LYB) recommended by Jeffrey Zekauskas of JP Morgan

On September 18, 2020, InvestorPlace contributor Chris Tyler approached his recipe from the technical chart perspective. Technical Analysis represents the opposite side of the coin from Fundamental Analysis, which is how most analysts approach the stocks they recommend. We don't have the knowledge or experience to cover technical analysis but if you read extensively, you will be introduced to it. Tyler says, "With some stocks carving out durable bottoming patterns, here are 3 Nasdaq stocks to buy:

- Netflix (NASDAQ:NFLX)

- Vertex Pharmaceuticals (NASDAQ:VRTX)

- First Solar (NASDAQ:FSLR)"

Unfortunately, we don't have enough space to reproduce the charts. Just be aware that technical analysis correlates price patterns to trends in stocks. Experts also argue that the fundamentals of a stock create the prices making up the charts that others examine—from a Technical Analysis perspective. Looking only at a company's earnings is called Fundamental Analysis. We suggest that both strategies are valuable, and you might want to review the technical charts of a stock you are researching.

Another approach is "meal kits" with an ingredients list and recipe. The premier example would be to purchase stock in Berkshire Hathaway, the company Warren Buffett founded. It includes wholly owned companies such as Geico Insurance and BNSF railway along with stock holdings like a mutual fund that includes banks and software companies. This allows you the luxury of someone else making the selections. This stable stock will continue even after its founder is no longer at the helm. Other able managers who are working alongside Buffett and Charlie Munger will take over. *Investor's Business Daily* recommended Berkshire Hathaway as a good way to ride the coattails of Buffett. It also added:

Under investment managers Todd Combs and Ted Weschler, Berkshire Hathaway has been increasingly sinking money into tech. It has taken large positions in established giants like Apple (AAPL), younger companies like the Brazilian payments company StoneCo (STNE), and Snowflake (SNOW), a new software IPO. Berkshire also snapped up a stake in *Amazon.com* (AMZN).

Berkshire Hathaway recently disclosed it has acquired stakes of slightly more than 5% in each of the five leading Japanese trading companies.

Mutual funds fill the same niche. Another great way to find stocks you might want to buy is to look at the top holdings of highly rated mutual funds. These can be found on the Yahoo Finance website. The chart on the following page shows the top ten holdings of Buffalo Discovery Fund (BUFTX), a mutual fund of mid-cap stocks. Top holdings are updated quarterly, so by the time you look at it, the numbers and holdings will have changed. If you invest across multiple mutual funds, you will achieve "pre-built" diversification.

The chart is from 2020, included for historical and example purposes only. Be sure to check out the current holdings.

Buffalo Discovery Fund (BUFTX)

* KSU (Kansas City Southern Railway) was acquired by Canadian Pacific Railroad in December 2021. Here's the caveat with any mutual fund.

Top 10 Holdings (16.08% of Total Assets)		Get Quotes for Top Holdings
Name	Symbol	% Assets
The Cooper Companies Inc	COO	1.81%
Take-Two Interactive Software Inc	TTWO	1.70%
Global Payments Inc	GPN	1.67%
CoStar Group Inc	CSGP	1.66%
IHS Markit Ltd	INFO	1.60%
Bio-Techne Corp	TECH	1.56%
MSCI Inc	MSCI	1.56%
Equinix Inc	EQIX	1.54%
Kansas City Southern	KSU	1.49%
SBA Communications Corp	SBAC	1.49%

This is an excellent one to own. Our friend used to own it along with individual stocks as shown below. If its performance appears to be lower than her individual stocks, bear in mind that she selected an annual distribution instead of rolling the fund's sales into more shares in the mutual fund. Profits are paid out from the fund's long- and short-term gains each year, thereby reducing the profit accruing in the owner's account.

Our Friend's Portfolio (date unknown)

			Value		Unrealized Gain/Loss	
Merrill Lynch CMA-Edge			$41,782		$18,957.11	83.26%
				Unrealized Gain/Loss		Value
				$Chg	%Chg	
BUFTX	BUFFALO DISCOVERY FUND	16.932	$26.45	$525.77	13.61%	$4,388.91
CMCSA	COMCAST CORP NEW CL A	100	$45.58	$2,489.78	120.38%	$4,558.00
CRM	SALESFORCE.COM INC	66	$244.53	$11,665.29	260.75%	$16,138.98
DIS	DISNEY (WALT) CO	50	$130.22	$1,238.30	23.49%	$6,511.00
FB	FACEBOOK, INC.	20	$254.82	$1,909.99	59.94%	$5,096.40
INTC	INTEL CORP.	100	$50.32	$1,127.98	28.89%	$5,032.33

Saturday is another slack day for financial news and a good time to search Yahoo Finance. Saturday, September 19, 2020, TipRanks reported on three extraordinarily high dividend stocks. TipRanks provides a link to each analyst's record. They cited:

- BlackRock TCP Capital (TCPC), recommended by JMP Securities analyst Christopher York. York has an out-perform rating on a stock that pays a 12.3% dividend and an $11 price target.

- PennyMac Mortgage (PMT), recommended by JMP Securities analyst Trevor Cranston. Cranston believes the stock will improve as the pandemic wanes. The stock recently paid a 9.1% dividend.

- Oaktree Specialty Lending (OCSL), followed by Christopher York of JMP Securities, pays over 8% dividend, and he expects a price target of $6

These are lesser-known stocks and have fewer shares outstanding, making them more volatile. But they may provide above average returns. They may be what we call *pantry stocks* until you have followed them for a period.

On the same day, TipRanks reported three recommendations on larger companies by analysts from Credit Suisse.

- Concho Resources (CXO), followed by Bill Janela, is ranked by Janela as a top pick with a price target 45% higher this year than its current $48.09 price. ConocoPhillips (COP) completed its purchase of CXO on January 15, 2021.

- Ares Management (ARES) is followed by Craig Seigenthaler. He indicates a 23% upside potential from its current $39.83 price.

- Carlisle Companies (CSL) has been recommended by analyst Adam Baumgarten who sees a 22% share price rise as the economy returns to normal with a price target of $150.

These companies are more widely followed by other analysts, so it would be possible to find other opinions. If you read these preliminary reports and believe they indicate suitable upside, consider adding them to your portfolio. One caveat is to be aware that if these analysts recommend a group of stocks from only one company, they are, by definition, not diversified.

Investment Guideline 6

Check blogs, websites, analysts' reports, television shows, financial magazines, and any other source you can access. Then analyze, investigate, and dig deeper into the companies that interest you. Finally, compare each of the companies to other oppotunities. Once you have done this numerous times and discovered what works best, you can more easily rank and separate them. Continually add to your knowledge base and hone your instincts for stocks that will turn into portfolio success.

Part III

Adding Extra Courses to the Meal

After Two or Three Years of Investing

Chapter 11

The Deep Future: Invest for the Unknowns

Don't spend time beating on a wall, hoping to transform it into a door.
—Coco Chanel

One day you will wake up in a world where all the expectations you hold and beliefs you rely on no longer apply. The COVID-19 Pandemic of 2020, like the Spanish Flu of 1918, flipped the world we live in like a pancake on a griddle. No one expected their jobs and their social interactions to be upended so quickly. Because we didn't expect the changes to last, some of us resisted wearing masks and staying away from bars or parties. The stock market reacted quickly. Many investors immediately assessed that the economy would be deeply impacted. The market suffered a temporary setback, and some stocks soared more than others because they could benefit as their products or services such as Zoom were in greater demand.

Investing is a response mechanism to the financial impacts on businesses affected by the pandemic. Investing too has a new dimension that we have not even begun to explore when things go wrong in the economy. Every investor must respond and face elements that reflect the challenging times that will always impact businesses.

We tend to believe that tomorrow will be like today. We plan our lives around the life we lived today and yesterday. Many children adopt the careers of one of their parents. How many preachers, doctors, lawyers, dentists, and teachers that you know had parents with the same career? Many lives reflect the models our parents established. Therefore, when bad news hits the market stocks soar or sink based on old reptilian instincts. But the calm investor doesn't push the panic button every time there is bad news. Just expect the unexpected to occur on any given day.

Own Some Gold or Precious Metals

To better insulate your portfolio from sudden turmoil, it should include precious metals. You can own them as jewelry, coins, small bars of metal, or stocks. Gold coins serve as both objects to enjoy and a store of wealth. We will suggest several investments in this category beyond gold and silver.

Your mind exists to be used and challenged. It is your greatest asset, an under-utilized gem, an uncut diamond waiting to shine. Think. Think more. Think harder. Think about your future.

As investors, by this point you should be building your portfolio. Let's say you own these stocks in a portfolio. It's all growth. If you need income stocks, buy a mutual fund, utility, or REIT that focuses on that. We want your portfolio to consist of stocks that can grow every year and increase your wealth. Assume you bought the following stocks* and own these now:

- CACI International
- Lam Research or Applied Materials
- Mercado Libre or Lexin Fintech
- Jazz Pharmaceuticals or BioMarin
- SYNNEX Corporation
- Google
- CrowdStrike or CyberArk
- Comcast or Disney
- Tractor Supply
- Advance Auto Parts or AutoZone or O'Reilly

*We are not suggesting you buy any of these without first doing research.

Now look into a thousand futures with an eye to adding stocks that are like insurance for things these stocks may not be able to account for. The first thing we recommend is an investment in precious metals. But there is greater risk than we are comfortable with suggesting any single security. Here is where a mutual fund that holds more than one stock would be the best choice.

The Good, the Bad, and the Ugly—Lessons Learned and Unlearned

What follows are lessons learned, and mistakes made. Investing and cooking sometimes result in mistakes. Embrace them, learn from them, and move on, but avoid a rearview mirror that you use only to berate yourself. Other times, an unexpected ingredient like Italian parsley added to a dish makes a memorable meal.

Read Peter Lynch's book *One Up on Wall Street*. He admits to making mistakes and missing opportunities, but overall, investing is like baseball—the more times you go to the plate the more likely you are to hit a home run. Lynch's premise is that you have the same capabilities, sometimes better insight, than the Wall Street experts. He says, "Twenty years in this business convince me that any normal person using the customary three percent of the brain can pick stocks just as well, if not better, than the average Wall Street expert." The world has changed a lot since 1989 when Lynch wrote this.

Again, we suggest that you buy twenty shares of a stock you like. Then buy twenty shares of a great company in a different kind of business. Add other stocks and additional shares of the ones you own as time and money permit. Monitor them all and build a watchlist or wish list. You can make your watchlist free at *Marketwatch.com* and at *Bloomberg.com*. Follow this suggestion even if you have a large sum to invest. This is your party. Invite guests but let them in one at a time as you get to know them. Ask them to leave if they misbehave. Then be patient for months or years.

An Example of Research and Waiting before Acting

Tableau Software—Taken Over by *Salesforce.com*

This is a history lesson of something we did right. This stock—Tableau Software—was first recommended by Merrill Lynch on December 10, 2014. It went onto our watchlist. The stock was selling for roughly $80 a share at the time of recommendation. Merrill Lynch analyst, Brad Sills and his team, reported, "We recognize that Tableau's stock is one of the most expensive in our universe, trading at 10x our Calendar 2015 revenue estimate. However, we believe the company will grow into this valuation (sustained 30% to 40% growth)." That ratio didn't look so wild from the perspective of 2020.

The target for the stock was $100. But the stock was not purchased into her account until January 1, 2018. We followed it for four long years. The company continued to grow but had some hiccups along the way. When we added sixty shares the price was $74.77 a share. It was risky to recommend a stock selling at high multiples of sales (not earnings) to a good friend. The plan was to hold the stock for a long time, but on August 1, 2019, *Salesforce.com* purchased Tableau software to enhance their own portfolio offerings. As of August 25, 2020, with the conversion of sixty shares into sixty-six shares of *Salesforce.com* and Salesforce's announced addition to the Dow Jones Index, the initial buy of $4,485.89 rose to $14,157.07. Now the fate of the initial investment depends on the strength of the total enterprise of *Salesforce.com*. On the down day of August 5, 2024, her *Salesforce.com* holding was down to $15,491.19, but as we wrap up the book in January 2025, her shares are worth over $22,000.

This stock belonged to a smaller portfolio she established at Merrill Lynch. That portfolio did not perform as well as the portfolio in the E*TRADE account. Any concerns about holding expensive stocks could have been avoided by buying an index, but we would not have learned anything, and this portfolio after five years beat the S&P 500 index. She started with $20,000 and today is worth $39,989.50 after withdrawing $4,000 during the last year. Even with mistakes, her smaller portfolio bounced back after it lost money in 2018. When you see a new house on your way to work, you don't know what setbacks and roadblocks the builder had to overcome. You only see the finished product. Buying stocks is like going to a lumber yard, selecting the materials, taking them to the site, and putting them together. It's not easy, and sometimes you're on the roof and imagine falling to the ground. Thankfully, it rarely happens.

Chapter 12

The Far Horizon:

Invest in What the World Will Look Like in Thirty Years

Future Shock

The present world you inhabit vanishes with the next step you take; each tomorrow erodes today. In 1970, Alvin Toffler wrote the book that defined the term "future shock" to indicate that the increasing speed of change would create in society a "shattering stress and disorientation" that most people could not cope with. We are amid it. The year 2020 contained every single element that will unsettle a society. Look how many company stocks soared that year because of changes in the economy. Some stocks went up because of increased demand for their services, such as Amazon, or due to recognition of the exponential increase in value of a product such as Zoom Video Communications. On the other end of the scale lie companies impacted by severe shocks. Those companies whose stock and business declined precipitously were airlines, cruise ships, petroleum, and education, to name a few.

We speculate at least half of the companies mentioned in Peter Lynch's book no longer exist. Companies get taken over, go bankrupt, or simply die like any living organism. We sometimes fail in the endeavors we undertake. But because our nation remains the land of opportunity, we spring back, we recover and move forward time after time. And it always gets better. We sometimes just can't see the light when it is dim. Your portfolio will decline sometimes to the point where you want to sell it all because the pain is real. Time after time we have learned to just stop looking and wait for the stock we own to recover. Currently, we own shares in some oil companies that continue to drop every single day. But we are still far away from utilizing renewable energy to the extent everyone wishes. Lower income people will be using combustion engine cars for many years into the future. Look how long people in Cuba have kept old American cars running. We hope for an electric, renewable future but until then oil will continue to be used. The CEOs of oil companies face a lot of criticism for past decisions. The future is impossible to see.

Who Can See the Farthest Ahead? Pharmaceutical Companies

As good-intentioned parents we learned that we couldn't be in two places, or more, at one time. The same is true with portfolios. You will juggle and waver among stocks that pay good dividends now, those with good future earnings and those where you think it will be a good idea to have a stake in the far-off future. Imagine you purchase AT&T (T) for the high dividend now. And Costco (COST) because it continues to grow and will grow to justify its high price-to-earnings ratio (PE), and you want to add a drug stock because there are tremendous possibilities among scientific healing discoveries.

COVID-19 has shown the need to have in place an infrastructure that can protect the body from assaults both known and unknown. Additionally, there are diseases that rob families of loved ones every day; diseases that still have limited or no known cure. We are not here to argue the ethical questions around who pays for drugs or procedures that save lives. We can only state the way the world works today. If AstraZeneca or Pfizer develops a new life-saving drug they will make, not millions, but billions. In 2011 Gilead Sciences (GILD) purchased Pharmasset for $12 billion (about $37 per person in the US) because it had developed a drug to cure hepatitis C. It was a deal that paid off quickly for Gilead but brought much condemnation because of the treatment price. But how many lives did it save or improve? If you have hepatitis and face compromise of your liver from the disease, is $84,000 for the twelve-week regimen too much for your life?

Cures for cancer and many other life-threatening diseases are a distinct possibility in the future. Scientists will be able to engineer more individual drugs for a single human's specific genetic profile. Someone will profit from these endeavors until we find a better way to pay for drug therapies. Until then you will have to read analysts' reports on drug companies and follow the news.

Large pharmaceutical companies develop and sell a variety of therapies and usually pay dividends, too. These are familiar names such as Merck, Eli Lilly, Johnson & Johnson, Pfizer and Bristol-Myers Squibb. Many people work in this industry—doctors (of course), scientists, and salespeople. They not only develop drugs on their own, but they look for smaller companies that are developing creative therapies and will buy or merge with another company to stay ahead. It's a must-own sector. Beyond these are hundreds of biotech companies that trade mostly on the NASDAQ exchange. These are riskier stocks. Immunomedics, Inc. announced a breast cancer drug with a unique delivery and target method and was almost immediately purchased by Gilead Sciences who had probably had their eye on IMMU for some time. These are stocks you will have to hold for a long time because they must undergo rigorous review by the Food and Drug Administration. These smaller stocks should be purchased through a biotech mutual fund. If you are a healthcare professional, you might look at these kinds of stocks.

There are several drug companies based in other countries that trade on the stock exchange. China develops many new drugs that, if effective, will be sold here. You will also see many European companies in advertisements for drugs such as GlaxoSmithKline, AstraZeneca, and Sanofi. The chart of almost every drug manufacturer forms an upward sloping curve. We would not say you can't go wrong, but generally the whole sector has rewarded investors. The one caveat is patience. Because development, approval and acceptance of drugs takes a long time, a drug company's stock can languish. Pfizer is a prime example. It has not grown much over the last five years. But we don't doubt their scientists are at work and could develop a life-altering drug at any time. Even Regeneron has not been straight up in the last five years. That chart looks like a flat-bottomed boat, but if you had bought shares at intervals each year when it turned up in 2020, you would have been rewarded.

Future Fuels

On September 25, 2020, Merrill Lynch said,

Steve Byrne [one of their analysts] along with the Thematic and other Sector research teams combined for a deep dive report on Hydrogen. Hydrogen, the first, lightest and most abundant element in the universe, could supply our energy needs, fuel our cars, heat our homes, and help to fight climate change. All while generating $2.5tn of direct revenues and $11tn of indirect infrastructure potential by 2050, while jumping 6x in volumes. They believe we are reaching the point of harnessing the element that comprises 90% of the universe, effectively and economically. Green hydrogen could be key in the fight against global warming, providing up to 24% of our energy needs by 2050, helping to cut emissions by up to 30%.

If you plan to pass your portfolio on to those you love, if you don't expect to be alive in 2050, then it still makes sense to learn about these things. Or find a mutual fund manager who invests in these things.

Merrill Lynch lists the work of several companies in this exciting sector. A Canadian company, Hydrogenics, is partially owned by Cummins [maker of truck engines]. It manufactures fuel cells of varying sizes that can produce electricity. Siemens and Toshiba along with many other familiar, and not so familiar, companies are exploring hydrogen opportunities.

Additionally, Bloom Energy (BE) manufactures, installs, and operates solid-oxide fuel cell generators, which convert natural gas and other fuels such as biogas into electricity without combustion. Nikola, in partnership with General Motors, is developing fuel cells for electric cars.

The Motley Fool on How Long To Hold Stocks

...[W]hen you buy an investment, we believe you should be looking a minimum of three years ahead, and guess what? If that's true of you, you're playing a different game entirely from most of the rest of the world. Most other investors are thinking about what to do in the next month, six months, or a year. A year feels like a long term for a lot of the people we watch on CNBC and others — Wall Street mutual funds turn over fully in one year. Clearly, we're playing a different game. We're playing the game the way it was meant to be played. Because after all, your gains are going to come from longer-term holdings. So, three years at a minimum is going to put you in a place where you're playing the game differently from others, and it's a game you're going to win.

Summary

The poet Wallace Stevens once said, "It can never be satisfied, the mind, never." Our world changes while we sleep as people are at work all over the world developing transforming technologies, plants, drugs—you name it. Be on your toes for new investments after you build your base portfolio and teach your heirs about these things. Then provide time for your investments to grow and blossom.

How to Avoid Big Trouble (or Disappointment)
Part 1

There is so much risk and so many unknowns when selecting stocks that you must walk away from some risks. A better option might be to look over the shoulder of a money manager who holds in her mutual fund the stock that interests you. You can only observe the top holdings of a mutual fund on *Finance. Yahoo.com*. You many have to invest in the mutual fund to see all the holdings. If it's a smaller stock, you might have to track in on your own watch list. The reason we say this is that stocks such as pharmaceuticals, for example, have long wait times between the time a drug is created and the approval process which may take years. To reduce risk, this is the point at which a sector mutual fund makes sense to own.

How to Avoid Big Trouble (or Disappointment)
Part 2

Also avoid stocks that are trading at new highs. They almost always come down. Wait for them to come down before you buy them. You will have to set a value that you are willing to pay for any stock then wait until it falls to your price. Several artificial intelligence stocks rose to new heights in mid-2024 but fell shortly after that. You must always stand upright at the helm of your ship filled with stocks and only take on cargo you approve.

Chapter 13

Pantry Stocks—Keeping an Eye Out for Your Next Ingredient (Purchase)

Pantries lined with shelves were built in houses before supermarkets came along. Mother stored things she would need at short notice. It was a sense of reassurance that something essential would always be close at hand.

> We maintain a watchlist of stocks we would not just like, but would love to own if we had more money. When it's earnings season we update our list. We have a file with notes and recommendations from analysts for these stocks. There are eleven primary sectors that stocks fall into (from *U.S. News and World Report.*)

The 11 Stock Market Sectors:

- Materials
- Industrials
- Financials
- Energy
- Consumer discretionary
- Information technology
- Communication services
- Real estate
- Health care
- Consumer staples
- Utilities

Market Capitalization—A Short Overview

Small-Cap—The definition of small-cap can vary among brokerages, but it is generally a company with a market capitalization of between $250 million and $2 billion USD.

Mid-Cap—Investors who want the best of both worlds might consider mid-cap companies, which have market capitalizations between $2 billion and $10 billion. Historically, these companies have offered more stability than small-cap companies yet confer more growth potential than large-cap companies.

Large-Cap—A large-cap stock has a market capitalization over $10 billion.

As a general rule, small-cap companies offer investors more room for growth but also confer greater risk and volatility than large-cap companies. We focus here on small-cap and mid-cap companies and suggest purchasing them. But large-capitalization stocks are more stable.

Materials

A company with a core business that takes some raw material or natural resource and, through a process, converts it into something more useful is almost always labeled a materials stock. Many chemical companies, mining companies, metals businesses and logging companies are in the materials sector, as are some oil and natural gas stocks. Major Examples: Rio Tinto (ticker: RIO), Vale S.A. (VALE) and Ecolab (ECL)

Companies We Put in Our Pantry:

Construction Partners [ROAD]

Construction Partners, Inc., an infrastructure and road construction company, provides construction products and services to public and private infrastructure projects. It offers construction of highways, roads, bridges, airports, and commercial and residential sites. The company provides a range of sitework construction services: site development, paving, constructing utility and drainage systems, and supplying hot mix asphalt, aggregates, ready-mix concrete, and liquid asphalt cement. It serves customers primarily in Alabama, Florida, Georgia, North Carolina, and South Carolina. The company was formerly known as SunTx CPI Growth Company, Inc. and changed its name to Construction Partners, Inc. in September 2017. Construction Partners, Inc. was founded in 2001 and is headquartered in Dothan, Alabama.

In March, 2020, the company acquired two hot-mix asphalt plants, located in Pensacola and Defuniak Springs, Florida. Among other things, the acquisition is expected to offer the following strategic benefits to the company:

The Pensacola plant represents the company's entry into a new market from which the company will be able to pursue a variety of public, private and Department of Defense projects.

The Defuniak Springs plant allows the company to service the Western Florida panhandle from a convenient location on the Interstate 10 corridor.

Both plants are located on or adjacent to aggregate rail terminals, facilitating the company's access to key inputs for the manufacture of hot-mix asphalt.

Our view is that this small-cap firm could be a company ready to go to the next level and expand beyond its regional footprint. That's why it's a pantry stock.

Vulcan Materials Company [VMC]

Vulcan Materials Company produces and supplies construction materials primarily in the United States. The company operates through four segments: Aggregates, Asphalt, Concrete, and Calcium. The Aggregates segment provides crushed stones, sand and gravel, sand, and other aggregates; and related products and services that are applied in construction and maintenance of highways, streets, and other public works, as well as in the construction of housing and commercial, industrial, and other nonresidential facilities. The Asphalt Mix segment offers asphalt mix in Alabama, Arizona, California, New Mexico, Tennessee, and Texas. The Concrete segment provides ready-mixed concrete in California, Maryland, New Mexico, Texas, Virginia, Washington D.C., and the Bahamas. The Calcium segment mines, produces, and sells calcium products for the animal feed, plastics, and water treatment industries. The company was formerly known as Virginia Holdco, Inc. and changed its name to Vulcan Materials Company. Vulcan Materials Company was founded in 1909 and is headquartered in Birmingham, Alabama.

In 2020, the House of Representatives passed an infrastructure bill for $1.5 trillion. These infrastructure initiatives would almost certainly boost sales for Vulcan Materials. The company ranks as the largest U.S. producer of construction aggregates such as crushed stone, sand, and gravel and is one of the top producers of construction materials including asphalt and ready-mixed concrete.

The states in which Vulcan operates are poised to generate 72% of the total U.S. population growth this decade. Nineteen of the 25 fastest-growing markets in the U.S. are served by Vulcan's operations. It makes sense that these areas will be a primary focus of federal infrastructure initiatives.

This is a Large-Cap company that could get a lot better. We view it as only a matter of time before infrastructure projects take a front-and-center position in the economy. No Harvard MBA will try to raise money to buy land and equipment to create another sand and gravel competitor. The permitting process is daunting in localities for new quarries where dynamite is used. It's a wide-moat company in our view.

Industrials

Although perhaps more loosely defined than some of the other stock sectors, industrial sector stocks tend to either be involved directly in the production of capital goods like aircraft, electrical equipment, industrial machinery and the like or the provision of transportation services and infrastructure. Many of America's most iconic blue-chip companies hail from the industrial sector, with many also playing a historic role in the evolution of U.S. society and American military might. Major examples: Boeing Co. (BA), Lockheed Martin Corp. (LMT), General Electric Co. (GE), Caterpillar (CAT).

Companies We Put in Our Pantry:

Howmet Aerospace [HWM]

Howmet Aerospace Inc. provides advanced engineered solutions for the aerospace and transportation industries in the United States, Japan, France, Germany, the United Kingdom, Mexico, Italy, Canada, Poland, China, and internationally. It operates through four segments: Engine Products, Fastening Systems, Engineered Structures, and Forged Wheels. The Engine Products segment offers airfoils and seamless rolled rings primarily for aircraft engines and industrial gas turbines. The Fastening Systems segment produces aerospace fastening systems. The Engineered Structures segment provides titanium ingots and mill products, aluminum and nickel forgings, and machined components and assemblies for aerospace and defense applications. The Forged Wheels segment offers forged aluminum wheels and related products for heavy-duty trucks and commercial transportation markets. The company was formerly known as Arconic Inc. Howmet Aerospace Inc. was founded in 1888 and is based in Pittsburgh, Pennsylvania.

The Aerospace Industry faces many hurdles currently. Howmet had a terrific rise in stock price in 2024 that will likely not be repeated in 2025. Long-term the stock has been a winner and has a bright future. This is one to purchase in small amounts during periods of weakness.

The Timken Company [TKR]

The Timken Company designs, manufactures, and manages engineered bearings and power transmission products and services worldwide. It operates in two segments, Mobile Industries and Process Industries. The Mobile Industries segment offers a portfolio of bearings, seals, and lubrication devices and systems, as well as power transmission components, engineered chains, augers, belts, couplings, clutches, brakes, and related products and maintenance services to original equipment manufacturers (OEMs) and end users of off-highway equipment for the agricultural, construction, mining, outdoor power equipment, and power sports markets; and on-highway vehicles, including passenger cars, light trucks, and medium- and heavy-duty trucks, also rail cars and locomotives. It also provides power transmission systems and flight-critical components for civil and military aircraft, which comprise bearings, helicopter transmission systems, rotor-head assemblies, turbine engine components, gears, and housings. This company offers its products under the Timken, Philadelphia Gear, Drives, Cone Drive, Rollon, Lovejoy, Diamond, BEKA, and Groeneveld brands. The company was founded in 1899 and is headquartered in North Canton, Ohio.

While Timken is over 100 years old, its products are up-to-date and no one else will likely go into these old-line businesses against them. Bearings literally make the world go around. It is the largest manufacturer of tapered roller bearings in the US and a leading global manufacturer of highly engineered bearings and power transmission products. It is not a wildly growing company but is mid-cap and provides a moderate upside with very little headache for the long run. We would buy it to balance out a portfolio.

Financials

There has probably never been so stark and empirical a rebuttal to the glib aphorism, "All press is good press," than financial sector stocks in the midst of the Great Recession. Banks were failing left and right, with many small-cap or mid-cap names going bankrupt or being bought out for pennies on the dollar. Even some of the biggest names on Wall Street—like Bear Stearns and Lehman Brothers—failed or were bailed out. A decade later, financials have still not recovered their reputation. The largest banks today are much more gargantuan than they were in the financial crisis.

But America owes a great deal, like it or not, to big banks. Historically, our banks, because they were big, enabled companies to grow. Bottom line, they swept up money into big piles where companies could back up their financial pickup trucks the same way homeowners go to the landscape center to load up on mulch. If the nation hadn't needed a lot of money, banks would not have proliferated the way they did. A large, successful nation needs large, successful financial institutions. Major examples of Financial Companies: Bank of America Corp. (BAC), Visa (V), PayPal Holdings (PYPL), Berkshire Hathaway (BRK.A, BRK.B).

Bank United [BKU]

BankUnited, Inc. operates as the bank holding company for BankUnited, a national banking association that provides a range of services to small and medium sized businesses and individual and corporate customers in the United States. The company offers deposit products, such as checking, money market deposit, and savings accounts; certificates of deposit; and treasury and cash management services. Its loan portfolio includes commercial loans, equipment loans, secured and unsecured lines of credit, formula-based loans, owner-occupied commercial real estate term loans and lines of credit, mortgage warehouse lines, letters of credit, SBA product offerings, trade finance, and business acquisition finance credit facilities; commercial real estate loans; residential mortgages; and other consumer loans. As of December 31, 2019, it operated through a network of 74 branches located in 14 Florida counties; and 5 banking centers in the New York metropolitan area. The company was formerly known as BU Financial Corporation. BankUnited, Inc. was founded in 2009 and is headquartered in Miami Lakes, Florida.

This mid-cap is poised to grow nicely. Its location could make it a takeover target as banks consolidate. It is a stock to watch but has not rewarded shareholders over the last five years.

C&F Financial [CFFI]

C&F Financial Corporation operates as a bank holding company for Citizens and Farmers Bank that provides banking services to individuals and businesses. The company's Retail Banking offers various services, including checking and savings deposit accounts, also business, real estate, development, mortgage, home equity, and installment loans. It also provides ATMs, internet and mobile banking, and debit and credit cards, as well as safe deposit box rentals, notary public, electronic transfer, and other customary bank services. This bank offers its services through its main office in West Point, Virginia, as well as through 25 Virginia branches. The company's Mortgage Banking segment provides various residential mortgage loans; originates conventional mortgage loans, mortgage loans insured by the Federal Housing Administration, and mortgage loans guaranteed by the United States Department of Agriculture and the Veterans Administration; and ancillary mortgage loan origination services for residential appraisals, as well as various mortgage origination functions to third parties. Its other segment offers brokerage and wealth management services; and insurance products. The company also provides title and settlement agency, and insurance services. C&F Financial Corporation was founded in 1927 and is headquartered in West Point, Virginia.

This company is literally in our backyards. It is definitely a small-cap business, but is solid and pays a very good dividend. It's been around so will likely continue to incrementally grow. We see it often on the way to work. You might call it a "pocket stock," but that's why it's in the pantry.

Energy

Businesses that provide the services and equipment allowing companies to extract sources of energy from the earth are considered a part of this sector, as are most of the companies that do the exploration, production, refining and marketing of fossil fuels like oil, natural gas and coal. Oilfield services companies are considered energy stocks, even if they just help locate a reservoir for a larger company or if they sell the equipment, fluids and materials necessary for horizontal fracturing, known as fracking. Major examples: Exxon Mobil Corp. (XOM), Schlumberger (SLB), Kinder Morgan (KMI), Halliburton Co. (HAL), Chevron (MRO).

Disclaimer

Jim Cramer calls oil the "new tobacco"—no one wants it but everyone uses it. This is a complex arena. There are a number of segments within energy now. You will find NextEra Energy that we like although it has a high per share price under Utilities. Energy consists of companies that provide services to drilling such as Haliburton and Schulmberger. There are companies that only refine crude oil into gasoline and other products such as Marathon Petroleum and Valero. Some companies' pipelines, only transport oil (warning these are often Master Limited Partnerships and can present some heartburn filing your taxes.) And finally there are the companies we love to hate: Exxon, Chevron, etc. But as an investor, you may want to consider one in your portfolio, but exercise caution so that you know what you are buying. In other words, investigate purchases in this area with more diligence than segments that seem golden such as technology.

TotalEnergies SE [TTE] (French)

TotalEnergies SE, a multi-energy company, produces and markets oil and biofuels, natural gas, biogas and low-carbon hydrogen, renewables, and electricity in France, rest of Europe, and internationally. It operates through five segments: Exploration & Production, Integrated LNG, Integrated Power, Refining & Chemicals, and Marketing & Services. The Exploration & Production segment is involved in the exploration and production of oil and natural gas. The Integrated LNG segment comprises the integrated gas chain, including upstream and midstream liquified natural gas (LNG) activities, as well as biogas, hydrogen, and gas trading activities. The Integrated Power segment includes generation, storage, electricity trading, and B2B-B2C distribution of gas and electricity. The Refining & Chemicals segment consists of refining, petrochemicals, and specialty chemicals, as well as oil supply, trading, and marine shipping activities. The Marketing & Services segment supplies and markets petroleum products. The company was formerly known as TOTAL SE and changed its name to TotalEnergies SE in June 2021. TotalEnergies SE was founded in 1924 and is headquartered in Courbevoie, France.

Most of the stocks in this category have been around for a long time. Total is in partnership with Apache developing an extensive oil reserve in Suriname but has also committed to more renewable energy in the future. It pays a significant dividend (subject to foreign taxes) while you wait.

Marathon Petroleum Company [MPC]

Marathon Petroleum Corporation, together with its subsidiaries, engages in refining, marketing and transporting petroleum products primarily in the United States. It operates through Refining & Marketing and Midstream. The Refining & Marketing segment refines crude oil and other feed stocks at its 16 refineries in the West Coast, Gulf Coast, and Mid-Continent regions of the United States; and purchases refined products and ethanol for resale. Its refined products include transportation fuels, such as reformulated gasolines and blend-grade gasolines; heavy fuel oil; and asphalt. This segment also manufactures aromatics, propane, propylene, and sulfur. It sells refined products wholesale, to customers domestically and internationally, buyers on the spot market, and independent entrepreneurs who operate primarily Marathon branded outlets. The Midstream segment transports, stores, distributes, and markets crude oil and refined products through refining logistics assets, pipelines, terminals, towboats and barges; gathers, processes, and transports natural gas; and gathers, transports, fractionates, stores, and markets natural gas liquids. The company also exports its refined products. As of December 31, 2019, it owned, leased, and had ownership interests in approximately 17,200 miles of crude oil and refined product pipelines. It is in the process of selling its Speedway retail arm. The company was founded in 1887 and is headquartered in Findlay, Ohio.

We like Marathon Petroleum [MPC] not to be confused with the drilling portion of the original company Marathon Oil [MRO] which is now part of Conoco-Phillips. It refines crude oil and pays a significant dividend which it is committed to maintaining. It will deploy the cash from the sale of its Speedway retail segment to improve efficiency.

Consumer Discretionary

Sometimes a name can say it all. Consumer discretionary is one of the more aptly named stock sectors: companies within it market their products and services to consumers, not businesses, and what they sell is generally bought with discretionary income; they're not hawking day-to-day necessities. Though admittedly a generalization, the sector is also sometimes known as consumer cyclical, which makes sense when you consider some of the industries it encompasses: automobiles, apparel, hotels, restaurants, leisure-related businesses and luxury goods, to name a few. Major examples: Carnival Corp. (CCL), Grubhub (GRUB), Lululemon Athletica (LULU), Party City

(PRTY).

MGM Resorts International (MGM)

MGM Resorts International, through its subsidiaries, owns and operates integrated casino, hotel, and entertainment resorts in the United States and Macau. The company operates through three segments: Las Vegas Strip Resorts, Regional Operations, and MGM China. Its casino resorts offer gaming, hotel, convention, dining, entertainment, retail, and other resort amenities. The company's casino operations include slots, table games, and race and sports book wagering. As of March 22, 2020, its portfolio consisted of 29 hotel and destination gaming offerings. The company also owns and operates Las Vegas Strip Resorts, Primm Valley Golf Club, and Fallen Oak golf course. Its customers include premium gaming customers; leisure and wholesale travel customers; business travelers; and group customers, including conventions, trade associations, and small meetings. The company was formerly known as MGM MIRAGE and changed its name to MGM Resorts International in June 2010. MGM Resorts International was founded in 1986 and is based in Las Vegas, Nevada.

Motley Fool Comments by Travis Hoium on Sept 1, 2020:

MGM has quietly built one of the most expansive online betting businesses in the U.S. and has valuable partnerships with the NBA, NHL, and MLB. Investors are betting that companies like DraftKings and Everi Holdings will build huge businesses as more betting moves online, but MGM Resorts has bigger brand names and a physical footprint these companies can't match. BetMGM is only available in five states right now (including Nevada), but it could expand nationwide over the next few years, and in states that require a physical presence, the lead may be insurmountable.

Today, legal online gambling and sports betting is a small business that's only available in a handful of states. But if that grows to most of the country over the next decade and goes more mainstream, it could be a multi-billion-dollar business in the U.S. Grand View Research even thinks online gambling could be worth $127.3 billion globally by 2027. MGM could end up being the market leader in U.S. online gambling and could even take the business worldwide. Pre-pandemic, this was already a strong cash-generating business, and with a market cap of only $12 billion, the upside potential from online gambling is too good to pass up.

We like it for the same reasons. Some people have qualms about investing in a company that makes its money from other people losing money. People gamble and if MGM doesn't provide the venue, then Penn National Gaming (PENN) or another company will. Consumers engage in potentially destructive behavior.

Lowe's Companies, Inc. (LOW)

Lowe's Companies, Inc., together with its subsidiaries, operates as a home improvement retailer in the United States, Canada, and Mexico. The company offers a line of products for construction, maintenance, repair, remodeling, and decorating. It provides home improvement products in various categories, such as appliances, paint, hardware, millwork, lawn and garden, lighting, lumber and building materials, flooring, kitchens and bathrooms, rough plumbing and electrical, seasonal and outdoor living, and tools. It also offers installation services through independent contractors in various product categories; extended protection plans; and in-warranty and out-of-warranty repair services. The company sells its national brand-name merchandise and private branded products to homeowners, renters, and professional customers. As of January 31, 2020, it operated 1,977 home improvement and hardware stores. The company also sells its products through websites comprising *Lowes. com* and *Lowesforpros.com*; and through mobile applications. Lowe's Companies, Inc. was founded in 1946 and is based in Mooresville, North Carolina.

Motley Fool Comments

Lowe's has consistently had to play catch-up with industry leader Home Depot. But the retailing chain is an attractive business in its own right. Some of its best qualities include a long track record of growth and profitability through every part of the growth cycle—and a dividend growth streak that's unmatched in the industry.

The performance gap with Home Depot often means the stock is available at a relative discount, both in terms of price-to-sales and price-to-earnings valuations. That factor lessens the risk that investors will overpay when seeking exposure to the home improvement industry.

We like Lowe's for the same reasons as Merrill Lynch recommends the company—people are continually upgrading or repairing their homes, and home prices generally continue to rise over time.

Appliances wear out, a window or door needs to be replaced, and new plants or mulch must be purchased each spring. Plus, what you don't see is that Lowe's updated their store distribution and logistics infrastructure some years ago which keeps the stores supplied. Peter Lynch would say to buy the stocks of the places where you shop if you think they are doing a superior job.

Information Technology

Arguably the premier stock market sector of the 21st century, information technology contains pretty much all the essential industries to today's internet-powered, device-driven world. Broadly speaking, software, hardware and semiconductors are the three pillars of this sector, which is geographically dominated by Silicon Valley. Major examples: Apple (AAPL), Cisco Systems (CSCO), Intel Corp. (INTC), Oracle (ORCL)

Disclaimer

There are hundreds of companies in this category to invest in. Trying to pick the next big winner is impossible, but here are two we believe will provide excellent returns no matter what the future holds. Everyone has a favorite. Buy the one that suits you best and hold on to it.

WIX.COM [WIX]

Wix.com Ltd, together with its subsidiaries, develops and markets a cloud-based platform that enables anyone to create a website or web application in North America, Europe, Latin America, and Asia. The company offers Wix Editor, a drag-and-drop visual development and website editing environment platform; Wix ADI that enables users to create a website for their specific needs; and Corvid by Wix to create websites and web applications. It also provides Ascend by Wix, which offers its users access to a suite of approximately 20 products or features enabling them to connect with their customers, automate their work, and grow their business; Wix Logo Maker that allows users to generate a logo using artificial intelligence; Wix Answers, a support infrastructure enabling its users to help their users across various channels; and Wix Payments, a payment platform, which helps its users receive payments from their users through their Wix Website. In addition, the company offers various vertical-specific applications that business owners use to operate aspects of their business online. Further, it provides a range of complementary services, including App Market that offers its registered users the ability to install and uninstall a range of free and paid web applications; Wix Arena, an online marketplace that brings users seeking help to create and manage a website, together with Web experts; and Wix App, a native mobile application, which enables users to manage their websites and Wix operating systems. As of December 31, 2019, the company had approximately 165 million registered users and 4.5 million premium subscriptions. The company was formerly known as Wixpress Ltd. *Wix.com* Ltd. was founded in 2006 and is headquartered in Tel Aviv, Israel.

Wix was added to our friend's portfolio at the end of 2018 when the market took a nose-dive before Christmas. It had been a watchlist stock for some time. It was a mid-cap stock at the time of purchase but has now joined the large-cap arena. What caught our eye at the time was its ability to allow users to easily customize their own websites. The pandemic required more companies to create or improve their websites. This trend will continue. Motley Fool advisors have recommended Wix three times since initially adding it to their list. It's almost a no-brainer.

While this is not a fly-into-the-sky company like Wix has been, it's a solid business that appears to be reasonably priced and within reach of many investors at this time. Its digital growth channel has good prospects, and not everyone has seen it yet.

Affirm Holdings, Inc. (AFRM)

Affirm Holdings, Inc. operates a payment network in the United States, Canada, and internationally. The company's platform includes point-of-sale payment solutions for consumers, merchant commerce solutions, and a consumer-focused app. Its commerce platform, agreements with originating banks, and capital markets partners enables consumers to pay for a purchase over time. The company has active merchants covering small businesses, large enterprises, direct-to-consumer brands, brick-and-mortar stores, and companies with an omni-channel presence. Its merchants represent a range of industries, including sporting goods and outdoors, home and lifestyle, travel and ticketing, electronics, fashion and beauty, equipment and auto, and general merchandise. Affirm Holdings, Inc. was founded in 2012 and is headquartered in San Francisco, California.

We like Affirm because the desire and need for consumers to buy now and pay later seems likely to grow as consumers feel more and more pressure to keep spending. The stock has had wide price swings over the last five years but should gradually improve going forward.

Datadog, Inc. [DDOG]

Datadog, Inc. operates an observability and security platform for cloud applications in the United States and internationally. The company's products comprise infrastructure and application performance monitoring, log management, digital experience monitoring, continuous profiler, database monitoring, data observability, universal service monitoring, network monitoring, error tracking, incident management, workflow automation, observability pipelines, cloud cost and cloud security management, application security management, cloud SIEM, sensitive data scanner, event management and CI and LLM visibility. Datadog, Inc. was incorporated in 2010 and is headquartered in New York, New York.

We were struck by Merrill Lynch's insight into DataDog that makes it a worthwhile holding for a very long time to come. This is a new company in a new space defined by Artificial Intelligence. Predictions about stocks are akin to writing on water. But we believe it will likely be taken over by another company in time.

Communication Services

One of the newest stock market sectors is communication services, which was formerly known as the telecom sector and was redefined in fall 2018. Decades of mergers and consolidation in the arena had made telecom an ultra-concentrated and practically irrelevant sector market-cap wise, and something else was happening, too. Efficient data transmission became increasingly important, and a torrential stream of popular new content that attracted billions of eyeballs demanded smooth and reliable distribution. Today, the communication services sector loosely refers to companies that offer such services (like traditional telecoms) and media and entertainment companies that facilitate communication but also have their own content. Major examples: Verizon Communications (VZ), Facebook (FB), Walt Disney Co. (DIS), Comcast Corp. (CMCSA)

Twilio Inc. [TWLO]

Twilio Inc., together with its subsidiaries, provides a cloud communications platform that enables developers to build, scale, and operate communications within software applications in the

United States and internationally. Its customer engagement platform provides a set of application programming interfaces that handle the higher-level communication logic needed for nearly every type of customer engagement, as well as enable developers to embed voice, messaging, and video capabilities into their applications. The company was founded in 2008 and is headquartered in San Francisco, California.

Twilio has had a wild ride during its short history. It's a good stock to watch. CFRA says, "We think TWLO's vast communication datasets create a competitive advantage for its AI capabilities." They provide a unique product/service for software development with embedded communications capabilities.

Comcast Corporation [CMCSA]

Comcast Corporation operates as a media and technology company worldwide. It operates through Cable Communications, Cable Networks, Broadcast Television, Filmed Entertainment, Theme Parks, and Sky segments. The Cable Communications segment offers cable services, including high-speed internet, video, voice, wireless, and security and automation services to residential and business customers under the Xfinity brand; and advertising services. The Cable Networks segment operates national cable networks that provide various entertainment, news and information, and sports content; regional sports and news networks; international cable networks; various digital properties, including brand-aligned websites, and engages in the cable television studio production operations. The Broadcast Television segment operates NBC and Telemundo broadcast networks, NBC and Telemundo local broadcast television stations, broadcast television studio production operations, and various digital properties. The Filmed Entertainment segment produces, acquires, markets, and distributes filmed entertainment under the Universal Pictures, Illumination, DreamWorks Animation, and Focus Features names. The Theme Parks segment operates Universal theme parks in Orlando, Florida; Hollywood, California; and Osaka, Japan. The Sky segment offers direct-to-consumer services, such as video, high-speed Internet, voice, and wireless phone services; and content services comprising operating entertainment networks, the Sky News broadcast network, and Sky Sports networks. The company also owns the Philadelphia Flyers, and the Wells Fargo Center arena in Philadelphia, Pennsylvania. Comcast Corporation was founded in 1963 and is headquartered in Philadelphia, Pennsylvania.

We think Comcast is a quiet juggernaut because of its cable operations which rise every year, subscribers say. Also, it has a foothold in Europe due to its acquisition of British Sky Group. Once the pandemic ends, Comcast's NBCU with Universal Studios will add significantly to revenue and profits. Good company to buy and add, buy and add over time.

Real Estate

One of the fastest-growing parts of the market in recent decades has been real estate, embodied most clearly by the rise of the real estate investment trust. An REIT is a tax-advantaged investment vehicle that can give retail investors a convenient way to gain easy exposure to the cash flow that comes with real estate ownership, but without the massive capital outlay required. All REITs except mortgage REITs are contained in this sector; mortgage REITs are found in the financial sector. Also, real estate development companies and management companies fall under this umbrella. Major examples: Redfin Corp. (RDFN), American Tower Corp. (AMT), Simon Property Group (SPG), Public Storage (PSA)

Alexandria Real Estate Equities, Inc. [ARE]

It is the first, longest-tenured, and pioneering owner, operator, and developer uniquely focused on collaborative mega campuses in AAA innovation cluster locations, with a total market capitalization of $27.7 billion as of June 30, 2020, and an asset base in North America of 43.0 million square feet ("SF"). The asset base in North America includes 28.8 million RSF of operating properties and 2.3 million RSF of Class A properties undergoing construction, 6.6 million RSF of near-term and intermediate-term development and redevelopment projects, and 5.3 million SF of future development projects. Founded in 1994, Alexandria pioneered this niche and has since established a significant market presence in key locations, including Greater Boston, San Francisco, New York City, San Diego, Seattle, Maryland, and Research Triangle. Alexandria Real Estate Equities is a real estate investment trust (REIT) based in Pasadena, California. It's the largest landlord in the US for laboratories and related offices. Its top companies by rent revenues include Amgen, Bristol-Myers Squibb, Celgene, Eli Lilly, Merck, Moderna, Novartis, Pfizer and Sanofi.

Neil George of InvestorPlace writes:

And those tenants pay. The most recent monthly rent collections were current for 99.4% of all leases. Moreover, Alexandria has 97% of its leases as triple-net. This means nearly all of its life science tenants pay rent as well as taxes, general upkeep, and insurance, which significantly reduces risks of unexpected costs and makes for a more dependable portfolio. Over 95% of leases have locked-end annual agreed base rent escalation agreements. That means, at minimum, Alexandria has inflation and cost control protections for its longer-term leases. And these agreements don't preclude additional rent increases as further negotiated.

We like it because if you have set up a laboratory with equipment and long-term testing on new drugs is underway, are you going to be looking to move very often? Unfortunately, it's not an inexpensive stock, but the growth record supports the investment thesis.

Extra Space Storage Inc. [EXR]

Extra Space Storage Inc., headquartered in Salt Lake City, Utah, is a self-administered and self-managed REIT and a member of the S&P 500. As of March 31, 2020, the company owned and/or operated 1,852 self-storage stores in 40 states, Washington, D.C. and Puerto Rico. The company's stores comprise approximately 1.3 million units and approximately 143.0 million square feet of rentable space. The company offers customers a wide selection of conveniently located and secure storage units across the country, including boat storage, RV storage and business storage. It is the second largest owner and/or operator of self-storage stores in the United States and the largest self-storage management company in the United States.

We suggest a look at this company because of its size and stability. It has not been in a growth mode recently but can consistently increase rents. Its customers have a lot of stuff. They are not going to make snap decisions about continuing to rent a unit because if they vacate, they either have to sell their belongings or find another place to hold them. Any REIT is a very long-term holding. Waiting for dividends and stock price to rise requires patience, but if it dips unexpectedly, it could become a strong buy.

Healthcare

Both on Wall Street and Main Street, healthcare is another sector that's been growing faster than the wider economy, accounting for an ever-larger percentage of Americans' expenses (and hopefully, portfolios). You've got two broad sides of healthcare when it comes to its classification in the stock market: the medical device manufacturers and medical services providers on one hand, and the actual biotech and pharmaceutical products – the drugs themselves – on the other. Major examples: Johnson & Johnson (JNJ), Pfizer (PFE), McKesson Corp. (MCK), Abbott Laboratories (ABT)

Veeva Systems [VEEV]

Veeva Systems Inc. provides cloud-based software for the life sciences industry in North America, Europe, the Asia Pacific, the Middle East, Africa, and Latin America. The company offers Veeva Commercial Cloud, a suite of multichannel customer relationship management applications, commercial data warehouse, allocation and alignment applications, master data management application, and data and services; and Veeva Vault, a cloud-based enterprise content and data management applications for managing commercial functions, including medical, sales, and marketing, also research and development functions, such as clinical, regulatory, quality, and safety. It provides professional and support services in the areas of implementation and deployment planning and project management; requirements analysis, solution design, and configuration; systems environment management and deployment services; services focused on advancing or transforming business and operating processes related to Veeva solutions; technical consulting services related to data migration and systems integrations; training on its solutions; and ongoing managed services that include outsourced systems administration. The company was formerly known as Verticals onDemand, Inc. and changed its name to Veeva Systems Inc. in April 2009. Veeva Systems Inc. was founded in 2007 and is headquartered in Pleasanton, California.

It has a unique position, but others such as *SalesForce.com* are building other options. All companies face innovations developed by competitors. If you have an instinct for medicine, this is a stock to get to know.

Chemed Corporation [CHE]

Chemed Corporation provides hospice and palliative care services to patients through a network of physicians, registered nurses, home health aides, social workers, clergy, and volunteers in the United States. It operates through two segments, VITAS and Roto-Rooter. The company also offers plumbing, drain cleaning, water restoration, and other related services to residential and commercial customers through company-owned and independent contractors, and franchised locations. Chemed Corporation was founded in 1970 and is headquartered in Cincinnati, Ohio.

While we are impressed with this stock, it has two drawbacks. It is an expensive stock and also operates a familiar plumbing segment. It has exhibited extraordinary growth over the past five years. Merrill Lynch writes in 2020 of Chemed:

We like the strong volume tailwinds for hospice and expect the rebasing to lift not only 2020 results but also drive higher acuity and thus above average pricing over time. We also like the solid cash flow generation at both Vitas and Roto-Rooter, combined with low leverage and a growing dividend.

More recently in 2024 they state:

After growing census 12-14% this year, Vitas expects to grow high-single (HSD) to low double digits (LDD) in 2025 and beyond given the continued robust recruiting and high retention. Having the capacity and stable workforce gives Vitas an advantage in getting long and short stay patients (length of stay is a key element of census growth).

Simply Wall Street states on *Finance.Yahoo.com*:

We like the trends that we're seeing from Chemed. The numbers show that in the last five years, the returns generated on capital employed have grown considerably to 33%. The company is effectively making more money per dollar of capital used, and it's worth noting that the amount of capital has increased too, by 35%. The increasing returns on a growing amount of capital is common amongst multi-baggers and that's why we're impressed.

We believe this is a stock worth watching and investigating.

Consumer Staples

Without the fruits of this sector, the human species would essentially go extinct. Food manufacturers and distributors; nondurable household goods; personal care products and beverages – the necessities of life that people keep needing and buying no matter how good or bad the economy is. You always need food, toilet paper, laundry detergent, shampoo, toothpaste, etc. The consumer staples sector is one of the most defensive, which means it can hold its own or even advance during a recession, but usually trails the market in expansions. Major examples: Coca-Cola Co. (KO), Colgate-Palmolive (CL), Procter & Gamble Co. (PG), Walmart (WMT)

BJ'S Wholesale Club Holdings, Inc. [BJ]

BJ's Wholesale Club Holdings, Inc., together with its subsidiaries, operates warehouse clubs on the East Coast of the United States. It offers perishable, edible grocery, general merchandise, and non-edible grocery products, as well as gasoline and other ancillary services. The company also sells its products through its website and mobile app. As of May 2, 2020, it operated 218 warehouse clubs and 145 gas stations in 17 states. The company was formerly known as Beacon Holding Inc. and changed its name to BJ's Wholesale Club Holdings, Inc. in February 2018. BJ's Wholesale Club Holdings, Inc. was founded in 1984 and is headquartered in Westborough, Massachusetts.

We like BJ's because it is a mid-cap growth retailer with a model similar to Costco—membership fees and sales of appealing items. In its favor is that consumer behavior increasingly shifts towards value & convenience. It is also not a high-priced stock so can easily be added to over time.

The Kroger Co. [KR]

The Kroger Co. operates as a food and drug retailer in the United States. The company operates combination food and drug stores, multi-department stores, marketplace stores, and price impact warehouses. Its combination food and drug stores offer natural food and organic sections, pharmacies, general merchandise, pet centers, fresh seafood, and organic produce; and its multi-department stores provide apparel, home fashion and furnishings, outdoor living, electronics, automotive products, and toys. The company's marketplace stores offer full-service grocery, pharmacy, health and beauty care, and perishable goods, as well as general merchandise, including apparel, home goods, and toys; and its price impact warehouse stores provide grocery, and health and beauty care items, as well as meat, dairy, baked goods, and fresh produce items. It also manufactures and processes food products for sale in its supermarkets and online; and sells fuel through its fuel centers. The company sells its products through its stores, fuel centers, and online platforms. The Kroger Co. was founded in 1883 and is based in Cincinnati, Ohio.

While the company faces many challenges, it is a resilient grocer and competitor. It is the largest conventional supermarket in the U.S., whose stock price has risen over the last year. It pays a small dividend but intends to grow it. It is better able to pass on price increases than most retailers.

Utilities

Utilities provide fundamentally necessary services like water, gas, and electricity to local communities and often wider regions. There are very high barriers to entry because of the capital-intensive and geographically limiting nature of their business, often making these companies natural monopolies. For this reason, they're highly regulated and their profitability is held in check by the government; the only water company for 1,000 miles couldn't decide to charge $20 per gallon for water, after all. Major examples: NextEra Energy (NEE), Duke Energy (DUK), Exelon Corp. (EXC), Dominion Energy (D)

Alliant Energy Corporation [LNT]

Alliant Energy Corporation operates as a utility holding company that provides regulated electricity and natural gas services in the Midwest region of the United States. It operates through three segments: Utility Electric Operations, Utility Gas Operations, and Utility Other. The company, through its subsidiary, Interstate Power and Light Company (IPL), primarily generates and distributes electricity, and distributes and transports natural gas to retail customers in Iowa; sells electricity to wholesale customers in Minnesota, Illinois, and Iowa; and generates and distributes steam in Cedar Rapids, Iowa. Alliant Energy Corporation, through its other subsidiary, Wisconsin Power and Light Company (WPL), generates and distributes electricity, and distributes and transports natural gas to retail customers in Wisconsin; and sells electricity to wholesale customers in Wisconsin. As of December 31, 2019, IPL supplied electricity to 490,000 retail customers and natural gas to 225,000 retail customers; and WPL supplied electricity to 480,000 retail customers and natural gas to 195,000 retail customers. It offers electric utility services to retail customers in the farming, agriculture, industrial manufacturing, chemical, and packaging industries. In addition, the company holds investments in various businesses, which provide freight services through a short-line railway between Cedar Rapids and Iowa City, Iowa; a barge terminal and hauling services on the Mississippi River; customized supply chain solutions; freight and logistics brokering services; and other transfer and storage services. Further, it owns a 347 megawatt (MW) natural gas-fired electric generating unit near Sheboygan Falls, Wisconsin; and a 225 MW wind farm located in Oklahoma. Alliant Energy Corporation was founded in 1917 and is headquartered in Madison, Wisconsin.

This utility has a firm footing in a supportive regulatory environment.

It grows modestly but consistently. It has no nuclear power generation and could expand its renewables. If owned, it would provide a consistent and stable stock to your portfolio.

Clearway Energy, Inc. (CWEN-A)

Clearway Energy, Inc., through its subsidiaries, acquires, owns, and operates contracted renewable energy and conventional generation, and thermal infrastructure assets in the United States. As of December 31, 2018, it held a contracted generation portfolio of 5,272 net megawatts (MWs) of wind, solar, and natural gas-fired power generation facilities, also district energy systems. The company owns thermal infrastructure assets with an aggregate steam and chilled water capacity of 1,385 net MW thermal equivalents; and electric generation capacity of 133 net MWs. Its thermal infrastructure assets provide steam, hot water and/or chilled water, and electricity to commercial businesses, universities, hospitals, and governmental units. The company was founded in 2012 and is based in Princeton, New Jersey. Clearway Energy, Inc. operates as a subsidiary of Clearway Energy Group LLC.

We like it because it is a small-cap stock. Because utilities are generally a century old, they are heavily regulated. The costs and benefits of regulation can be debated but regulation generally creates market stability. Clearway has more flexibility and operates in an exciting area for future growth. It has several classes of stock, so investigate before you buy, but generally the class A shares are the ones for public investors. It pays a dividend.

Chapter 14

Some Final Pieces to the Puzzle

The Fun Sector of Investing—Leisure Companies

There are certain aspects to the market that have a uniquely American flavor. Americans have—rightly or wrongly—always claimed to be different, and history and experience suggest that in economic and market terms there could be some truth to that.

American Exceptionalism as a social science theory is beyond the scope of this book, one element of that theory is what we call the "fun factor." All humans like to have fun, but many Americans have more disposable income to spend on recreational endeavors than citizens in some other parts of the world. The stereotype of this might be huge yachts, or million-dollar country club memberships. But our focus is more on the ordinary fun factor that the most Americans can access.

Our concept of this phenomenon includes mud boggers who purchase their four-wheel drive vehicles from the auto sector, video gamers who purchase their games from the tech sector, outdoor enthusiasts who purchase their gear from a variety of specialists in the retail sector, all those who travel who purchase hotel rooms and plane tickets from the tourism and travel sectors. Taken in combination, the fun sector is one of the largest in the economy and is, to a degree, permanent, although not fully recession-proof.

Here are some ordinary examples:

- Polaris (PII) used to make snowmobiles as a major manufacturing item; now they also make "neighborhood electric vehicles" and other recreational vehicles and related items, as well.

- Electronic Arts (EA) began in 1982 as an experimental home computer game agenda and now has roughly ten thousand employees and more than fifteen billion dollars in annual revenue.

- As of this writing, Dick's Sporting Goods (DKS) is more successful post-coronavirus than it was pre-coronavirus.

As you continue to develop and diversify your portfolio, all the rules we've outlined still apply, but dipping into the fun sector is another recipe with a solid performance record. Several well-known companies firmly occupy the fun sector, such as Disney (DIS) and Netflix (NFLX) along with airline, gaming, and resort companies. Additionally, Thor Industries (THO) builds recreational vehicles. We will cover two of these. Think of things you do for fun and ask yourself who owns them. They may be part of a larger corporation such as Comcast who owns Universal Studios and theme parks.

Norwegian Cruise Lines Holdings (NCLH)

Norwegian Cruise Line Holdings Ltd. operates as a cruise company in North America, Europe, the Asia-Pacific, and internationally. The company operates the Norwegian Cruise Line, Oceania Cruises, and Regent Seven Seas Cruises. It offers cruise itineraries to Scandinavia, Russia, the Mediterranean, the Greek Isles, Alaska, Canada and New England, India and the rest of Asia, Tahiti and the South Pacific, Australia and New Zealand, Africa, South America, the Panama Canal, the Caribbean, and Harvest Caye. As of February 20, 2020, the company had twenty-eight ships with approximately 59,150 berths. It distributes its products through retail/travel advisers, international travel advisers, and onboard cruise sales channels, as well as meetings, incentives, and charters. The company was founded in 1966 and is headquartered in Miami, Florida.

NCLH's stock was crushed in 2020. It did not resume services until sometime in 2021. But, if you had the money and the stomach for it, 2021 would have been the time to purchase it. Always look for stocks that no one else owns and see if you can wait until things improve. Recall the previous quote from Baron de Rothschild, "Buy at the sound of cannons." 2020 was that time.

The Walt Disney Company (DIS)

The Walt Disney Company, together with its subsidiaries, operates as a global entertainment company. The company's Media Networks segment operates domestic cable networks under the Disney, ESPN, Freeform, FX, and National Geographic brands; and television broadcast networks under the ABC brand, as well as eight domestic television stations. Its Parks, Experiences and Products segment manages theme parks and resorts, such as Walt Disney World Resort in Florida; Disneyland Resort in California; Disneyland Paris; Hong Kong Disneyland Resort; and Shanghai Disney Resort; Disney Cruise Line, Disney Vacation Club, National Geographic Expeditions, Adventures by Disney, and Aulani, a Disney resort and spa in Hawaii, as well as licenses its intellectual property to a third party for the operations of the Tokyo Disney Resort in Japan. The company's Studio Entertainment segment produces and distributes motion pictures under Walt Disney Pictures, 20th Century Fox, Marvel, Lucasfilm, Pixar, Fox Searchlight Pictures, and Blue Sky Studios banners. Disney develops, produces, and licenses live entertainment events; produces and distributes music; and provides post-production services, including visual and audio effects. Its Direct-to-Consumer & International segment operates international television networks and channels comprising Disney, ESPN, Fox, National Geographic, Star, and Other India Channels; direct-to-consumer streaming services consisting of Disney+, ESPN+, Hotstar, and Hulu. It provides branded apps and websites, such as Disney Movie Club and Disney Digital Network, and streaming technology support services. The company was founded in 1923 and is based in Burbank, California.

Disney's motion picture and theme park segments were curtailed by the pandemic in 2020. But it will spring back. The company's stock has not been as hard hit as Norwegian Cruise Lines stock, but it has suffered a decline. This too would be a good stock to own for the next twenty years. It's almost 100 years old but has been constantly kept up to date by acquisitions. NCL is a well-regarded and well-run company. Although specific "tips" will come and go, the overarching philosophy about what to look for remains the same.

You want a stock that's been around for at least a little while, and you must be able (in your own mind) to put faith and trust in the company. As an investor, you're not buying one person, but the whole company. And like any relationship, you want to know what you're getting into.

Target remains an excellent example, even with the ups and downs of the market. It's a company that is rich in capabilities and diversities that insulate it against long-term struggles. It also has a management philosophy that has adapted to unpredictable forces, and they always recover quickly from any setback.

Investors must adopt a long-term horizon, like Warren Buffet who says, "[My holding time is] forever!" Many companies come back from the brink of disaster; others don't; one must study what makes them different from each other.

You want to identify "forever" companies. Is Nvidia a forever company, for example? You'll need to do your research to decide for yourself, but we think it will be.

Tools and Information You Could Need

We encourage you to read, research, and identify any term or concept you don't understand. There are too many to cover them all here, but analysts are familiar with all the nuances of company metrics and include them in their recommendations.

Price-to-Earnings Ratio

The definition of the term from *Investopedia.com* states:

> *The price-to-earnings ratio (P/E ratio) is the ratio for valuing a company that measures its current share price relative to its per-share earnings. The price-to-earnings ratio is also sometimes known as the price multiple or the earnings multiple. P/E ratios are used by investors and analysts to determine the relative value of a company's shares in an apples-to-apples comparison. It can also be used to compare a company against its own historical record or to compare aggregate markets against one another or over time.*

To obtain the ratio, simply divide the price of the stock by the last twelve months of earnings. We feel that most definitions, by themselves, provide no clarity to investors. On September 29, 2020, Apple had a P/E of 34 on *Finance.Yahoo.com*. The P/E is listed on the summary page just above the EPS (earnings per share) for the past twelve months. The numbers you will see are followed by a notation, "TTM"—for Trailing Twelve Months. In 2024 it showed Apple earned $3.30 for the previous twelve months and the price was roughly $114 a share. Divide the share price by the EPS and that's the P/E. Because Apple is a fast-growing company, it will likely earn more money next year. Stock prices are projected onto expected future earnings. One analyst projected Apple's earnings per share to be about $4.50 a share in 2022, making its P/E about 21 then. That's what drives the price of stocks. The faster a company is expected to grow, the higher its P/E ratio. On the same day CSX Railroad's P/E was about 21 since its earnings were not projected to grow at the same rate as a company like Apple.

You will need to read and follow this metric over time. Different industries carry different PEs. Different companies within the same industry carry differing P/Es based on expected growth. The general rule is that if two companies are similar, then the one with the lowest PE has the best potential price appreciation.

Dividend Reinvestment Plans—Drip

A dividend reinvestment plan (DRIP or DRP) is a plan offered by a company to shareholders that allows them to automatically reinvest cash dividends in additional shares of the company on the dividend payment date. Dividend reinvestment plans are typically commission-free and offer a discount on the current share price. If you plan to hold a stock that pays a dividend for a long time, then this is an option to consider. If the dividend is minimal, it may not make sense to add this wrinkle into your portfolio.

Return On Invested Capital (ROIC)

Return on invested capital (ROIC) is a calculation used to assess a company's efficiency at allocating the capital under its control to profitable investments. The return on invested capital ratio gives a sense of how well a company is using its money to generate returns. If you invest large sums of money, you will likely need to calculate it for yourself, but those of us buying small numbers of shares can rely on the analyst.

ROIC is a measure that Berkshire Hathaway utilizes for its massive investments. In the 2007 shareholders letter, Warren Buffett wrote about ROIC:

> *Now let's move to the gruesome. The worst sort of business is one that grows rapidly, requires significant capital to engender the growth, and then earns little or no money. Think airlines. Here, a durable competitive advantage has proven elusive ever since the days of the Wright Brothers.*

Companies with high ROIC are Apple, Facebook, Visa and similar companies that don't have to build buildings, buy planes, or hold inventory.

You Can't Time the Market

We subscribed to the Andrew Slather email newsletter, which is free. They cite a study that covered 1926 to 1993 by Sanford Bernstein and Company. The study found that "93% of the time, returns in the stock market averaged about 0.01%." That sounds shocking on its surface, but they found that most of the gains came from the seven percent of time when the market went up. They say, "You can try to time the market and make short term gains fast. That means you can try to jump out and into the market and hope to be right about the timing and capture those returns—but you'll only have a 7% chance of doing it."

It's not market timing; it's time in the market is a well-known Wall Street adage. Invest for the long, long term. Over time you will discover that dividends make up a greater and greater portion of your gains. Sit back and try to enjoy the ride. Continue to buy stocks on a regular basis. Doing the things that we recommend will provide a positive outcome.

Chapter 15

Where to Find the Stocks
and Which Stocks to Buy

Only buy something that you'd be perfectly happy to hold if the market shut down for ten years. —**Warren Buffett**

A simple rule dictates my buying: be fearful when others are greedy, and be greedy when others are fearful. —**Warren Buffett**

Where To Find Stocks To Consider

We have mentioned a few ways to find stocks in the previous chapters. But there are still more ways to uncover the names of good investments. There are thousands of individual stocks, mutual funds, index funds, represent an ideal type of asset with which to build a diversified portfolio. We will only talk about individual stocks. You can learn about other investments on your own.

The first place to look is on the home page of *Finance.Yahoo.com*. Every day they name a stock that some analyst or brokerage recommends. Also, a headline that says a famous investor just bought or sold a particular stock. Now the world knows about them. Investigate them, add them to a watchlist.

Do not purchase any stock until you have researched it. You can look at any brokerage company's list of mutual funds, search for what they have researched, and which stock in the fund they think will lead the pack. Put the symbol in *Finance.Yahoo.com* and click on "Holdings" and it will show their top holdings.

Of course, you can use analysts' reports provided by your brokerage or buy subscriptions to newsletters of independent research companies such as Morningstar or CFRA Research. Both are excellent. There are many others as well. We often use Merrill Lynch. They tout stocks they think will have near-term catalysts. By the time you read the report and see what it's selling for, the stock price will likely have already made an upward or downward move. Put those that sound promising on your watchlist.

Some Mutual Fund Examples

Below are the symbols of some outstanding mutual funds to see what they are buying and what has made them successful. These are rated by Morningstar as four- and 5-star top performers:

T. Rowe Price Capital Appreciation I (TRAIX)
(Closed to new investors but you can buy some of the stocks they hold.)
Top 6 Holdings (18.03% of Total Assets)

Name	Symbol	% Assets
Microsoft Corp	MSFT	5.42%
Alphabet Inc Class A	GOOGL	2.70%
Amazon.com Inc	AMZN	2.69%
NVIDIA Corp	NVDA	2.57%
UnitedHealth Group Inc	UNH	2.56%
Danaher Corp	DHR	2.09%

T. Rowe Price All-Cap Opportunities Fund (PRWAX)
Top 9 Holdings (36.81% of Total Assets)

Name	Symbol	% Assets
Apple Inc	AAPL	7.03%
NVIDIA Corp	NVDA	6.10%
Microsoft Corp	MSFT	5.97%
Amazon.com Inc	AMZN	4.24%
Meta Platforms Inc Class A	META	2.99%
Alphabet Inc Class C	GOOG	2.81%
Visa Inc Class A	V	2.71%
Eli Lilly and Company	LLY	2.65%
Netflix Inc	NFLX	2.31%

T. Rowe Price Diversified Mid Cap Gr I (RPTTX)
Top 10 Holdings (15.80% of Total Assets)

Name	Symbol	% Assets
CrowdStrike Holdings Inc Class A	CRWD	2.47%
Apollo Global Management Inc Class A	APO	1.92%
The Trade Desk Inc Class A	TTD	1.62%
Palantir Technologies Inc Ordinary Shares - Class A	PLTR	1.52%
Cencora Inc	COR	1.49%
Ross Stores Inc	ROST	1.40%
Spotify Technology SA	SPOT	1.40%
Cintas Corp	CTAS	1.38%
Copart Inc	CPRT	1.30%
DexCom Inc	DXCM	1.30%

ClearBridge Select I (LBFIX)
Top 10 Holdings (35.99% of Total Assets)

Name	Symbol	% Assets
NVIDIA Corp	NVDA	6.83%
ServiceNow Inc	NOW	5.43%
Apple Inc	AAPL	4.55%
Microsoft Corp	MSFT	3.55%
MercadoLibre Inc	MELI	3.34%
KKR & Co Inc Ordinary Shares	KKR	2.77%
Copart Inc	CPRT	2.67%
Performance Food Group Co	PFGC	2.67%
Casey's General Stores Inc	CASY	2.16%
HealthEquity Inc	HQY	2.02%

Franklin Mutual International Value Z (MEURX)
Top 10 Holdings (30.61% of Total Assets)

Name	Symbol	% Assets
BP PLC (British Petroleum)	BP.L	3.62%
Novartis AG Registered Shares	NOVN.SW	3.51%
Roche Holding AG	ROG.SW	3.47%
Schlumberger Ltd	SLB	3.00%
BNP Paribas SA	BNP.PA	3.00%
Shell PLC	SHEL.L	2.96%
DBS Group Holdings Ltd	D05.SI	2.78%
Deutsche Telekom AG	DTE.DE	2.78%
Olympus Corp	7733.T	2.76%
Deutsche Bank AG	DBK.DE	2.73%

Franklin Mutual Global Equity I (SMYIX)
Top 10 Holdings (25.70% of Total Assets)

Name	Symbol	% Assets
NVIDIA Corp	NVDA	4.83%
Microsoft Corp	MSFT	4.51%
Apple Inc	AAPL	4.47%
Amazon.com Inc	AMZN	2.34%
Alphabet Inc Class C	GOOG	1.71%
Meta Platforms Inc Class A	META	1.68%
Alphabet Inc Class A	GOOGL	1.68%
Novo Nordisk A/S Class B	NOVO-B.CO	1.59%
Invesco Shrt-Trm Inv Treasury Instl	TRPXX	1.52%
Applied Materials Inc	AMAT	1.37%

Portfolios We Designed

Portfolio 1

Recipe for Pot Roast Dinner	Recipe for Stock Portfolio	Category/Sector	Percent
4 pounds boneless chuck roast	Ameriprise Financial (AMP)	Financials Sector	18%
6 medium potatoes, peeled and quartered	Nvidia (NVDA)	Information Technology	12%
6 to 8 whole carrots	Howmet Aerospace (HWM)	Industrials	11%
2 to 3 cups beef stock	United Healthcare (UNH)	Healthcare	10%
1 onion, chopped	BJ's Wholesale (BJ)	Consumer Discretionary	10%
2 cloves garlic, minced	MercadoLibre (MELI)	Consumer Discretionary	10%
2 teaspoons olive oil	Barrick Gold (GOLD)	Materials Sector	6%
1 teaspoon salt	Hubspot (HUBS)	Information Technology	6%
2 Bay Leaves	Construction Partners (ROAD)	Industrials	5%
½ teaspoon freshly ground black pepper	Deere & Company (DE)	Industrials	5%
Red wine	Capital One (COF)	Financials Sector	4%
Parsley	ConocoPhillips (COP)	Energy Industry	3%
			100%

Portfolio 2

Recipe for Lasagna	Recipe for Stock Portfolio	Category/Sector	Percent
1 pound sweet Italian sausage	Amphenol (APH)	Information Technology	15%
¾ pound lean ground beef	Apple (AAPL)	Information Technology	12%
12 lasagna noodles	Tractor Supply Co. (TSCO)	Consumer Discretionary	10%
16 ounces ricotta cheese	Ralph Lauren Corp. (RL)	Consumer Discretionary	10%
¾ pound mozzarella cheese, sliced	Ollie's Bargain Outlet (OLLI)	Consumer Discretionary	10%
¾ cup grated Parmesan cheese	Royal Bank of Canada (RY)	Financials Sector	10%
½ cup minced onion	Grupo Aeroportuario del Pacífico (PAC)	Industrials	5%
2 cloves garlic, crushed	AerCap Holdings N.V. (AER)	Industrials	5%
1 (28 ounce) can crushed tomatoes	AECOM (ACM)	Industrials	5%
2 (6.5 ounce) cans canned tomato sauce	Nucor Corporation (NUE)	Industrials	5%
4 tablespoons chopped fresh parsley, divided	Compass Group PLC (CPG.L)	Consumer Discretionary	4%
1 ½ teaspoons dried basil leaves	Fox Corporation (FOXA)	Communication Services	3%
1 ½ teaspoons salt, divided, or to taste	Pinnacle West Capital (PNW)	Utilities	2%
1 teaspoon Italian seasoning	CSX Corporation (CSX)	Industrials Sector	2%
¼ teaspoon ground black pepper	Lululemon Athletica Inc. (LULU)	Consumer Discretionary	2%
			100%

Portfolio 3

Recipe for Johnny Marzetti Casserole	Recipe for Stock Portfolio	Category/Sector	Percent
8 ounces rotini pasta	COSTCO (COST)	Consumer Discretionary	15%
1 pound ground beef	Microsoft (MSFT)	Information Technology	12%
½ pound bulk mild Italian sausage	AbbVie (ABBV)	Healthcare	12%
¾ cup chopped onion	Eaton Corporation plc (ETN)	Industrials Sector	10%
¼ cup chopped celery	Chubb Insurance (CB)	Finance	10%
1 clove garlic, minced	Hubbell Incorporated (HUBB)	Industrials	10%
1 tablespoon minced green bell pepper	International Bus Machines (IBM)	Information Technology	6%
salt and pepper to taste	Netflix (NFLX)	Communication Services	6%
1 (15 ounce) can tomato sauce	Meta Platforms, Inc. (META)	Communication Services	5%
1 (14.4 ounce) can diced tomatoes	Booz Allen Hamilton Holding Corporation (BAH)	Industrials	5%
2 cups shredded Italian cheese blend	Alexandria Real Estate Equities, Inc. (ARE)	Real Estate Sector	4%
1 ½ cups shredded sharp Cheddar cheese	Merck (MRK)	Healthcare	3%
salt and pepper to taste	Alamos Gold Inc. (AGI)	Materials Sector	2%
			100%

Portfolio 4

Recipe for Benihana Hibachi Chicken and Hibachi Steak	Recipe for Stock Portfolio	Category/Sector	Percentage
4 boneless, skinless chicken breasts halves	McKesson (MCK)	Healthcare	15%
6 cups bean sprouts	Applied Materials (AMAT)	Information Technology	12%
2 medium zucchini	Linde Plc (LIN)	Industrials	12%
2 cups sliced mushrooms	Proctor & Gamble (PG)	Consumer Staple	10%
1 large onion	GE Aerospace (GE)	Industrials	10%
2 tablespoons vegetable oil	The Southern Company (SO)	Utilities	9%
6 tablespoons soy sauce	American International Group, Inc. (AIG)	Financials Sector	6%
2 tablespoons butter	Lineage (LINE)	Real Estate Sector	6%
2 teaspoons lemon juice	XPO, Inc. (XPO)	Industrials	5%
3 teaspoons sesame seeds	Palantir Technologies Inc. (PLTR)	Information Technology	5%
salt	MDU Resources Group, Inc. (MDU)	Utilities	4%
pepper	Agnico Eagle Mines Limited (AEM)	Materials Sector	3%
mustard sauce	Hewlett Packard Enterprise Company (HPE)	Information Technology	2%
ginger sauce	Blue Owl Capital Inc. (OWL)	Financials Sector	1%
			100%

Portfolio 5

Outback Steakhouse Alice Springs Chicken	Recipe for Stock Portfolio	Category/Sector	Percent
4 boneless, skinless chicken breasts halves	Walmart (WMT)	Consumer Discretionary	15%
8 slices of bacon, cooked	GE Vernova Inc. (GEV)	Utilities	11%
2 cups sliced mushrooms	Reinsurance Group of America, Incorporated (RGA)	Financials Sector	11%
1 cup shredded cheddar cheese	TotalEnergies SE (TTE)	Energy Industry	10%
1 cup shredded Monterey Jack cheese	Nvidia (NVDA)	Information Technology	10%
1 tablespoon vegetable oil	Fidelity Diversified International (FDIVX)	Mutual Fund	9%
2 tablespoons butter	Fixerv, Inc. (FI)	Information Technology	6%
2 teaspoons finely chopped fresh parsley	Wells Fargo & Company (WFC)	Financials Sector	6%
Paprika	O'Reilly Automotive, Inc. (ORLY)	Consumer Discretionary	5%
salt	Amazon.com, Inc. (AMZN)	Consumer Discretionary	5%
pepper	Visa Inc. (V)	Financials Sector	4%
Honey Mustard Marinade:			
1/2 cup Grey Poupon	Chevron (CVX)	Energy Industry	2%
1/2 cup honey	D.R. Horton, Inc. (DHI)	Consumer Discretionary	2%
1-1/2 teaspoon vegetable oil	Vulcan Materials Company (VMC)	Building Material	2%
1/2 teaspoon lemon juice	Freeport-McMoRan Inc. (FCX)	Materials Sector	2%
			100%

Chapter 16

A Vision of Fewer People without Wealth

The only thing worse than being blind is having sight but no vision.
—Helen Keller

I am not a ward of America; I am one of the people who built this country.
—James Baldwin

This book is about increasing wealth for you and your family! It is about becoming an economic chef, with mastery of basic recipes/investments, and then inspiration for more complex endeavors. It is a chance for another capitalist success story, yours. It is an avenue for a different outcome both for you and for our nation as we will describe. Money is the basic ingredient in all these recipes, like water from the kitchen tap. It is not, however, available to everyone for the purpose of investing.

This book is not about sociology per se, but you've read far enough to know that part of our plan for this book is to help people become more independent financially, more risk-savvy, and more interested in enhancing their own economic success beyond their job earnings. Given the historical economic inequalities in America, often associated with capitalism itself, this is easier said than done.

The cultural truth is that the Stock Market is an iconic idea that has long represented wealth, prestige, power, influence, elitism, and control. Some people see Wall Street as a place for rich, young elites to play with other people's money, making themselves rich in the process. Even though this is a stereotype and should be avoided in general, there is just enough truth to it that the bigger problem must be addressed.

Let's get right to the point: we suggest that Congress and the president .pass a law(s) that provides $1,000 of seed money into a personal investment account for everyone who makes less than $50,000 a year up to ten years, even if they already, by some miracle, have such an account. They must have filed an income tax return in the last year—no tax return, no seed money. It is a privilege to pay taxes in this country for the benefits we receive. The recipient must be at least twenty-five years old and a citizen (like the requirements laid out in the Constitution to become a member of the House of Representatives.) Such an idea is not unprecedented. President Abraham Lincoln signed the Homestead Act on May 20, 1862. On January 1, 1863, Daniel Freeman made the first claim under the Act, which gave citizens up to 160 acres of public land provided they live on it, improve it, and pay a small registration fee. The government granted more than 270 million acres of land while the law was in effect. The grantee could provide proof of what they did to improve the land and obtain the deed to the land. The new law might specify that the account must be invested in an S&P 500 Index fund. An individual could then add to the investment or just deposit the dividends into their checking account. Individuals would apply for these grants through the financial entity that holds the account. The financial entity, such as Merrill Lynch or E*TRADE, would be responsible to see that the original $1,000 remains in the account. If an account holder passes away, the money reverts to the government. The goal is to incentivize individuals to invest by leading them to discover how wealth can grow. It would be a boon to the entire economy and nation. We offer too little of this kind of incentive. There are many tax-abatement laws to provide incentives for property development, but they are limited to those with enough money to invest already. This would be a bootstrap grant. A bill like this would provide hope for those with no hope, incentives for those with none, and a boost to those who are already trying to improve their lives. Some would even be lifted off their feet onto a higher path.

Another reason to explore this incentive is to provide retirement funds for older Americans. According to Nicholas Eberstadt, life expectancy has risen by three months per year for almost two centuries. If it continues, there will be expectations of living for a century. Social Security began as a pyramid model. Current wage earners would pay into the system until they turned sixty-five. But until the 1960s, most people, especially men, did not live much beyond sixty-five and few lived into their seventies. As retired people lived longer, the law was changed to raise the amount of income that was subject to Social Security tax and increase the retirement age. The Social Security Trust Fund has been able to meet the payouts. But it is projected to run out around 2035. The laws regulating Social Security will need to change to manage funding for this benefit.

What is ahead is an inverted pyramid as birth rates decline. Potentially, more people could be receiving Social Security benefits than those being taxed to fund it. Therefore, it's quite likely, Congress will require workers to provide more personal funding for their retirement. But a starter fund as we are describing makes its own argument.

Congress will not even raise the minimum wage in this nation without a near revolution. A law like this would give citizens an incentive to elect only representatives, senators, and a president who would support such a bill. We, the people, need to use a louder voice.

Once, there existed laws that enabled the construction of the Transcontinental Railroad. The Land Grant Act of 1850 provided 3.75 million acres of land to the states to support railroad projects. Railroads got rich because of taxpayer support in the nineteenth century. Why can't some support today go to private citizens, enabling them to become stronger partners in the fabric of society? Consumers and citizens are the employees of many wealthy public and private companies who could provide the support to transform this nation in a meaningful way. Capitalism needs to become a two-way street. Too often it has provided more money for those who already have it. This is one small way to channel some public money to the underappreciated lower-economic classes. It would also help maintain the middle class.

Is this a gamble for the Federal government? Not when you consider that in 2020 [when we began writing this book] we all received an economic stimulus check for $1200 from the government during COVID-19 out of thin air. Our proposed grants, like the recent bank bailouts, would be small considering the drastic measures taken during the Great Depression to level the economy and stimulate prosperity. Plus, those who already own stocks would benefit immediately if more demand for stocks caused the value of existing portfolios to rise. It's one of the rare win-win situations we can imagine.

Sufficient evidence exists to talk about generational poverty in America. Tax and inheritance rules intended to level the playing field or tax the wealthy have shifted to assist the wealthy when passing on their resources within the family. For example, according to research by the Tax Policy Center, "At death, deferred and unrecognized capital gains are exempted from income tax altogether because heirs reset the basis of the assets to their value on the date of death." Low-and-middle income taxpayers generally are unable to accumulate enough wealth to benefit from some of the laws that can only be used by those with a lot of wealth. There is an argument that these factors are a normal part of the "system."

Here's how it works today. If you sell one of your stocks and realize a profit, you are taxed on that profit. The tax rate you pay on a sale is determined by the length of time you have held the stock. Stocks owned less than a year are considered short-term, and any profits are taxed at your overall tax rate as if they were ordinary income. But there is no social security tax on these. Long-term gains are taxed at the 15% tax bracket rate. Upon your death you can transfer any stock to an heir. They receive it at the cost basis of that moment in time, as mentioned above, and do not pay taxes on the profit accumulated while you were alive. If our friend holds onto her Apple stock until she passes away, her daughter will, by rule of law, escape paying 15% tax on any gain. What a great way to pass along additional wealth to her heirs without them having to pay taxes on the money her mother made! Some say that the stock market, like capitalism itself, is arguably stacked against people with less affluence. It is specially designed in such a way that information is synonymous with money itself.

We are trying to make the argument that this information/money is available to everyone, regardless of education level, gender, creed, etc. The truth is that inequality is a problem in our society. If you are born into a wealthy family, the odds favor your continued prosperity. You can build some level of wealth or add to your basic income/net worth like our friend did by making a ten-year plan and sticking with it. Many need a hand to get off the struggle bus and board the wealth bus. There's no doubt that America is a fabulously wealthy country, but where is that wealth stored and controlled? According to a post on the blog *dqydj.com* [Don't Quit Your Day Job] entitled "How Many Millionaires Are There in America?"

We estimate that there are 14,814,453 millionaires in the United States. A million-dollar net worth for a household is the 88.24% wealth bracket in the US in 2016: 11.76% of all households. Note: for this stat and the subsequent ones, we are only discussing household data.

Poverty is such a big topic that we simply cannot summarize it cogently in a paragraph or two. *The Nation* estimated in 2013:

> *Roughly 46.5 million people live at or below the government-defined poverty line—which, as most who work with the hungry, the homeless, the uninsured, and the underpaid or unemployed know, is itself an inadequate measure of poverty.*

More recent surveys from the 2018 Census Bureau provide a figure of 38 million living in poverty, which they define as $25,465 for a family with two adults and two children. Whatever the most accurate number is, it's appalling. No one plans to be poor, but living with an income under $25,465 whatever the size of the family is poverty. For this income bracket, our advice to save early and often and then save some more is a near impossibility.

Making a cookbook for the basic or new investor must address the cultural stereotypes and the economic reality of disparities in America. There is a reason that the wealthiest Americans continue to benefit from the market across generations and that people in lower income brackets do not. Upper-income families own stocks or other assets and the rest of us don't own enough. It is a form of institutionalized inequality that has been perpetuated in our government structures, our embrace of consumerism, and our tacit acceptance of the way things are today.

This book is about making money, and making your money work for you, but it is not about getting rich, which takes a longer time than the horizon we lay out. It's about building a solid, non-speculative portfolio at whatever level you currently can. It's about generating some success and experience wherever you are now. It's about practicing patience, changing your perspective, and seeing beyond the moment. It's the same thing as the story of early American immigrants: working off an indenture; gaining fifty acres and building a log cabin; leasing more land and building a frame house; planting bigger crops; and eventually passing that along to the next generation. Except that this is the twenty-first century version.

Not everyone, of course, was fortunate enough to come to America (or live) under the same circumstances. Some came as slaves. Some were already here as natives and were pushed off their own land and persecuted. In the twenty-first century, however, most of us have an equal "pioneer" kind of access to the stock market. The market doesn't have to be a repeat of past mistakes we've made.

Obviously, this book, and even some of the extensive financial literacy resources that already exist, can't eliminate a structural problem. But it can continue to chip away at the issue, and you, by reading this book and beginning to cook in the Wall Street kitchen, will be doing your part to lift your family slowly into greater financial security.

We understand that each of us must advocate for ourselves financially to survive and thrive in our culture. But you can be out for yourself, and thereby, also help everyone else. In essence, our participation rather than our political beliefs or empathy is what could make such a paradigm possible and successful. We want more Americans to become savvy investors and participants in America's wealth.

Would millions of Americans saving more hurt the consumer economy? Initially, it might be true. But everything we say is about deferred gratification. Demand would possibly wane when people start saving but could return, as those savings and dividends rise. The economy would not be impacted in the long run.

Is Investing Gambling?

Many people who lived through the Great Depression believed owning stocks was gambling. They saw or heard of people impacted by their losses in the stock market. The market was down for a long time. The nation did not pull out of the Great Depression until massive government spending during World War II created more jobs than could be filled. The nation took on a tremendous amount of debt to build, equip and supply millions of soldiers, Marines, pilots, and sailors. There is a preconceived notion that investing is a rich person's avocation. In the following generation, a lot of parents believed that only when they could accumulate more money than they needed could they invest in stocks. They might say, "If I had money to play with, I would buy Ford or General Motors." If your parents never owned a share of stock, then they could not advise you on such a strategy. Fortunately, most workers were reintroduced to investing through their 401(k)s. Congress passed the Revenue Act of 1978, which included a provision added to the Internal Revenue Code—Section 401(k)—that allowed employees to avoid being taxed on deferred compensation. As a result, investment companies and mutual funds promoted investing in stocks with 401(k) plans and IRAs.

But the notion of stocks as gambling persists especially when the market surprises us with wild price gyrations. Inherently, if we don't understand it, we compare the stock market to our experience of going to Las Vegas and losing money. Many of us never get to Las Vegas, but the gambling moniker sticks. Remember when you buy stocks you are purchasing shares in a company with customers, employees, sales and earnings, and sometimes a building. If it makes your family feel more comfortable, buy stocks in local retailers, such as Dollar Tree, or the railroad, such as Union Pacific, that goes through town so you can see and touch what you own a part of. Investing is good for you in the long run.

Peter Lynch in *One Up on Wall Street* devotes an entire chapter to "Is This Gambling, or What?" With a proposal such as ours, many voters would say we are encouraging people to speculate with taxpayer money. So, maybe the stipulation should be added that the money can only go into an index fund. Index funds are still buffeted by market fluctuations. Since we can find no evidence that markets do not eventually recover, although it can take time, this would simply shore up the argument that investing is not gambling or speculation. Lynch points out how the severest market decline of the 1980s—the market crash of October 19, 1987—recovered quickly. "But two months later the stock market had rebounded, and once again stocks were outperforming both money-market funds and long-term bonds. Over the long haul they always do." Any precipitous drop seems to provide evidence of gambling, but stocks are not chips stacked on a roulette table. Lynch says, "People who succeed in the stock market also accept periodic losses, setbacks, and unexpected occurrences. Calamitous drops do not scare them out of the game." Of course, we take issue with his use of the word "game" in this case because investing is not gambling.

There is also a conversation about the need for and nature of wealth. Although it is beyond the scope of this book to go too far into depth on the topic, it is fair to point out that some religious and cultural traditions eschew wealth, seeing its aggressive accumulation as unseemly, or even wrong. It is our contention that the system of markets and capitalism that currently exist in the U.S. and globally have many good things associated with them; and some not so good, like profound income inequality, poverty, and lack of equal educational opportunity. The important point is that we are part of that system whether we like it or not, and we can share in its successes. Depending on decisions made beyond our pay grade, others who haven't previously done so can also benefit. There is a potential win/win that doesn't have to involve everyone buying yachts and million-dollar country club memberships. Rather all income levels can benefit from being able to pay for their children's education and being able to afford reasonable housing.

The biblical parable of the talents irresistibly comes to mind. The servant who hid his one talent in the ground was punished. The two who took a risk and invested were rewarded with even more. This book is for those who want to use their ingredients to cook something delicious, not let the spices and raw material languish in the cabinet unused.

Summary

Start Small, Stay Smart (and humble) and Add to Your Holdings

Short cuts make long delays.

—J.R.R. Tolkien

The Hero's Journey

This story has a happy ending. You will succeed. You will become more secure. Your finances will be more balanced. The hero in the hero's journey goes through many dark times but always wins in the end. Investing is a process and the hardest game on the longest field you will ever encounter. Do not flinch; do not give up the fight. We use the game analogy because it feels like a game when you're losing. When all the "good" stocks are going up and the ones you own are not, you will want to run away or quit. But downturns are always temporary. You will feel the losses more deeply than the gains. Just stay on the field and continue doing your best. Because the entire nation wins in the long run, only the stocks of the most poorly run companies ultimately fail to produce gains of some sort. We've said it before, don't compare your portfolio to the indexes. The indexes are compositions of every company in their defined universes. You can't own that many stocks. Always be happy with what you own. Get rich slowly, build your portfolio brick-by-brick over the span of time you choose. Allow a company's prospects to flower and bear fruit. As Peter Lynch once said, "Everyone has the brain power to make money in stocks. Not everyone has the stomach."

You can establish a winning portfolio with what may at first seem like average companies. Just remember that the employees who work for you get up every morning planning to perform at their highest levels. Superior management gets more from their employees than even the employees expect sometimes. You have every advantage. Set your eyes on the prize.

For any single action you make, no one will judge you. It will not be posted on Facebook or the internet for all to see. The other thing to do is to wait for one or two more earnings reports before deciding whether to sell at a loss or add more. This is what the hero does when facing her opponents. She either shoots one of her last arrows in the quiver or waits for a better shot. During the hero's quest, the hero will fail several times before mastering her fate. You might think of your stocks as your troops or the citizens of the kingdom you reign over. When you succeed, every one of them will cheer. It's up to you, the hero of your own story, to create your vision of your quest.

Another way to look at it might be to think of yourself as a homesteader on the plains or on the Oregon Trail to California. You arrive at a barren portfolio. You must bring in ideas, water/money and provide the effort and energy to make it produce. It will take some time to build the flourishing farm you envisioned when you set out. Tolkien also said, "The wide world is all about you: you can fence yourselves in, but you cannot forever fence it out." Forging ahead is the only path now.

All the pundits and advisers and even friends will tell you that managing your own portfolio will end in destruction and heartache. Isn't that what those who remain in the castle tell the hero? In the hero's journey, the hero lives in the ordinary world and gets a call to go on an adventure. The world that the hero encounters—the stock market—seems wild and strange, but the hero succeeds in overcoming all challenges along the way. Carry some of that energy into this investing endeavor.

Why You Will Be Successful

In what seems like an old book now, *The Search for Excellence* by Thomas J. Peters and Robert H Waterman, Jr., written in 1982, is a wealth of information for investors. It's helpful both for assessing companies and assessing yourself as the CEO of your portfolio. In Chapter 3, Man Waiting for Motivation, they discuss employee motivation studies from the twentieth century. We will summarize as best we can. They quote an unnamed manager from General Motors who said, "Our control systems are designed under the apparent assumption that 90 percent of the people are lazy ne'er-do-well, just waiting to lie, cheat, steal, or otherwise screw us. We demoralize 95 percent of the workforce who do act as adults by designing systems to cover our tails against the 5 percent who really are bad actors."

The authors (Peters and Waterman) point out that most organizations encourage risk taking but punish the smallest failures. But we encourage you to be your own CEO and set the rules. How will you treat yourself when the stock you pick goes down or stays the same? The stock market is a hard taskmaster. Peters and Waterman use the sales quota system of IBM as an example, saying that IBM's targets were more achievable for salespeople than other companies that set targets so less than half of their salespeople could meet them. However, those companies did worse than IBM. They basically said companies must make their employees feel like winners not losers. You must create your winning mindset as well. We believe failures are opportunities by another name.

They also cite studies that told participants they could not do well:

> *In one experiment, adults were given ten puzzles to solve. All ten were the same for all subjects. They worked on them, turned them in, and were given the results at the end. But, in fact, the results were fictitious. Half of the exam takers were told they had done well, getting seven out of ten correct. The other half were told they had done poorly, getting seven out of ten answers wrong. Then they were all given another ten puzzles (the same for each person). The participants who had been told they had done well in the first round did better in the second, and the other half did worse.*

We become what we tell ourselves we will become. Tell yourself you will prosper.

They contend that just as children in school excel when praised by their teachers, adults will perform better if they come from an experience of past personal success. So, praise yourself for your efforts every step of the way. If things don't go well, ask yourself where the problem might be. But give yourself a long runway to accomplish your targets rather than run away if your portfolio declines. We are telling you if you research a stock and read an analyst's report, you will likely succeed. Also, buy small quantities so that you can develop a self-correction plan. Time is on your side. As we wrap up this book around August 5, 2024, we are witnessing some of our stocks, soon to be *your* stocks, lose significant value. Everyone is looking for the next big decline (bear market) right now. You cannot *ever* time the market. With your new mindset and enthusiasm, along with this book, you are prepared to invest for yourself and your family.

Investment Guideline 7

Sometimes the stock of a fine company, one that is doing everything right, will decline and then decline some more. When that happens, do a reassessment, and if you conclude there is nothing wrong with the company, but the wider world says sell it, then step up to the plate and buy some more. If you own a good stock that you think has declined too much, *buy it in the trough*. All those sawtooth marks on stock charts represent times when a good stock went down but nothing was wrong. Look at a long-term chart for MercadoLibre. As we write this on November 24, 2024, Motley Fool contributor, Josh Kohn-Linquist said:

Even after this incredible run, however, I have been waiting for a chance to add to my MercadoLibre position, as I believe the company's best days are still ahead of it. The company recently reported solid earnings, but the stock still dropped 10%, potentially providing an excellent opportunity to continue adding to my MercadoLibre position at a discount.

Soon, the stock was up 4.32% at 2 pm EST to $2,091.57.

Guy and Jack's Investment Guidelines

Investment Guideline 1

Imagine you are buying stock for a daughter, son or grandchild so they can buy their first home. Buy reasonably priced, normally growing stocks. Expect your stocks to hit singles and doubles. Do not expect a homerun.

Then be patient. Don't give up and sell it too quickly.

Investment Guideline 2

When choosing between two equally well-recommended companies, pick the one with the most valuable human capital. The companies doing well today are high-tech and pharmaceutical. It's not by accident. Their employees add more value and are harder to replace.

Corollary: If you're in a hurry or can't decide, buy a highly rated Big Blue-Chip stock since they have developed a lot of human capital over the years.

Investment Guideline 3

Don't invest in stocks for short-term gains. When asked what his holding period was for a stock, Warren Buffett said *forever*. A longer than three-year holding period allows management's strategy to demonstrate it efficacy. It helps an investor avoid the peaks and valleys of stock prices. Stocks, like bread, need to be left alone to rise. In most cases, if a stock doesn't rise after three years, it will likely be around the same price as when you bought it. Then decide if it needs more time or it's time to harvest the funds and find another one.

Investment Guideline 4

"Play your game, don't play their game," a friend, Mark Y, said about how he manages his portfolio. Don't be driven out of your position if the market goes down precipitously. We've made that mistake too often and lost over and over. Think of yourself as an artist. Stocks are your paint pallette.

Investment Guideline 5

Be grateful you were able to save some money to participate in the greatest economy with the most opportunities for future gains. It will get better from wherever your stocks are at this moment. Consumers' wants can never be satisified; that's why they will return again and again to purchase cars, clothes, Christmas gifts, and computers. You won't go broke with a diversified portfolio. It just sometimes feels that way!

Investment Guideline 6

Check blogs, websites, analysts' reports, television shows, financial magazines, and any other source you can access. Then analyze, investigate, and dig deeper into the companies that interest you. Finally, compare each of the companies to other oppotunities. Once you have done this numerous times and discovered what works best, you can more easily rank and separate them. Continually add to your knowledge base and hone your instincts for stocks that will turn into portfolio success.

Investment Guideline 7

Sometimes the stock of a fine company, one that is doing everything right, will decline and then decline some more. When that happens, do a reassessment, and if you conclude there is nothing wrong with the company, but the wider world says sell it, then step up to the plate and buy some more. If you own a good stock that you think has declined too much, *buy it in the trough.* All those sawtooth marks on stock charts represent times when a good stock went down but nothing was wrong. Look at a long-term chart for MercadoLibre. As we write this on November 24, 2024, Motley Fool contributor, Josh Kohn-Linquist said:

Even after this incredible run, however, I have been waiting for a chance to add to my MercadoLibre position, as I believe the company's best days are still ahead of it. The company recently reported solid earnings, but the stock still dropped 10%, potentially providing an excellent opportunity to continue adding to my MercadoLibre position at a discount.

Soon, the stock was up 4.32% at 2 pm EST to $2,091.57.

About the Authors

Jack Trammell, Ph.D. is an award-winning author of more than two dozen books and hundreds of articles, poems, and essays. His work has appeared around the globe and in hundreds of venues. He is a popular speaker on many subjects ranging from disability and social history to the art of writing. He is also Associate Professor and Chair of the Sociology, Criminal Justice, and Human Services Department at Mount Saint Mary's University in Maryland. In 2014, Jack ran for Congress in the Virginia 7th District (Eric Cantor's district) in the "Two Professors Race" which received international media attention. Jack also is active in his community, where he serves as Deacon in his church, on several non-profit boards, and as an election volunteer.

He lives on a small farm in Virginia with his wife Audrie, and occasionally, many grandchildren.

His most recent collaboration with Guy Terrell is *Civil War Richmond: The Last Citadel* (The History Press; late 2020 release).

Guy Terrell, M.B.A., M.S. co-authored *A Short History of Richmond* and *The Fourth Branch of Government: We the People* with Jack Trammell. He has also published poems in *Tar River Poetry Review* and *Streetlight*. He earned his B.A. at Hampden-Sydney College, an M.B.A. from George Mason University and an M.S. in Information Systems from Virginia Commonwealth University. He is retired from a career in project management and systems analysis.

www.ingramcontent.com/pod-product-compliance
Lightning Source LLC
Chambersburg PA
CBHW042120190326
41519CB00031B/7560